themodernjapanesegarden

themodernjapanesegarden

introduction by shunmyo masuno

photography by michael freeman   text by michiko rico nosé

TUTTLE PUBLISHING Boston • Rutland, Vermont • Tokyo

the**modern**japanese garden

Published in 2002 by Tuttle Publishing, an imprint of
Periplus Editions (HK) Ltd., with editorial offices at
153 Milk Street, Boston, Massachusetts 02109.

First published in 2002 by Mitchell Beazley, an
imprint of Octopus Publishing Group Ltd.

ISBN 0-8048-3437-7

CIP catalogue copy for this book is available on
request.

Executive Editor: Mark Fletcher
Executive Art Director: Christie Cooper
Project Editor: Michele Byam
Design: Geoff Borin
Contributing Editor: Richard Dawes
Production Coordinator: Alex Wiltshire
Indexer: Phyllis Van Reenen

Distributed by
North America
Tuttle Publishing
Distribution Center
Airport Industrial Park
364 Innovation Drive
North Clarendon, VT 05759-9436
Tel: (800) 526-2778
Tel: (802) 773-8930
Fax: (800) 329-8885

Japan
Tuttle Publishing
RK Building, 2nd Floor
2-13-10 Shimo-Meguro
Meguro-ku
Tokyo 153 0064
Tel: 81-35-437-0171
Fax: 81-35-437-0755

Southeast Asia
Berkeley Books Pte. Ltd.
130 Joo Seng Road
#06-01/03 Olivine Building
Singapore 368357
Tel: (65) 280-1330
Fax: (65) 280-6290

Set in Helvetica

Printed and bound in China by
Toppan Printing Company Limited

contents

introduction

shunmyo masuno

What is a modern garden? Clearly, it is not sufficient to say that it is just what is being designed now. We have to put it in context, and, as these are Japanese gardens, context is everything. In Western art (and gardens are for us an art, as we shall see), modern has become identified with Modernism, and more recently with Post-Modernism. Modernism was an innovation and a challenge to the existing order, and carried with it, particularly in architecture, the rejection of decoration and ornament. Post-Modernism arose as a challenge to all of this, particularly to functional design. In recent years there has been a similar wave of experimentation in gardening throughout the world. Old principles are being challenged, and in many cases nature itself is rejected. Here too, in Japan, we are experimenting, but one of the essential differences, I think, is that we still refer carefully to our traditions of garden design.

The oldest tradition of all is that the garden represents nature, and that nature, since prehistoric times, has been regarded as sacred. This is true for both Shinto and Buddhism, although the two religions differ in their views. The earliest beliefs, which evolved into Shinto, were in the *kami* – sacred powers – who set foot at particular natural sites, often a stone called an *iwakura*. So the point of contact for man was the sacred natural enclosure, and this was the beginning of the garden. To this day Shinto shrines incorporate nature, by keeping a natural habitat in which there are sacred plants, such as the *sakaki* (*Cleyera japonica*), and cordoned precincts of pebble beds.

Buddhism, too, attaches a special importance to gardens, as in the re-creation of the paradise of Amida, the Buddha of the West. When Zen Buddhism arrived in Japan from China in the thirteenth century, a special concept of the garden came with it, which profoundly affected the Japanese. As a Zen priest I find it strange, and unsatisfactory, that

❯

The sacred rock of Waroza-ishi, inscribed with Sanskrit characters, lies in Kumano, an area of Japan with many natural features sacred in Shinto. In this name "za" indicates that the rock is regarded as a seat for gods – a place where they touch the Earth.

❮

In Shinto tradition, the sacred precinct surrounding the plain wooden architecture of the shrine is laid with white stones, as here at the Auxiliary Sanctuary of Tsuchinomiya at Isé. This simple, austere design has exerted a profound and continuing influence on Japanese gardens.

At the Imperial Shrine at Isé, Shinto priests add a branch of the evergreen shrub *sakaki* (*Cleyera japonica*) to the *karahitsu* box containing food for the gods. This plant, similar to a camellia and from the same family, is sacred in Shinto.

The Zen garden of Ryumontei, or Dragon Gate, at Gion-ji temple in Mito, was designed by Shunmyo Masuno. The prominent upright stone on the left represents the priest Shinetsu telling the Chinese parable of the carp to an audience that includes the Vice-Shogun Mitomitsukuni, who is symbolized by the pyramidal stone near the far wall.

The key ingredients in the dry-stone garden are pebbles and white sand, divided by a pattern of tiles sunk into the earth. A fallen camellia flower is left where it lies. In the Japanese aesthetic, the overhanging branches of flowering trees are expected to contribute, in their natural fashion, to the design of the garden, and camellias are valued because the flowers fall intact.

Zen has for many people in the West become a shorthand expression used only in the context of design, a synonym for minimal. It is much more than that, and has led to the formation of our unique culture. So much of Japanese culture, art, and the performing arts such as the tea ceremony, black-ink *sumi* paintings, Noh theatre, calligraphy, pottery, and gardens are inconceivable without Zen. The aesthetic awareness of the Japanese, who generally love simplicity and profound subtlety, almost personifies the spirit of Zen, and it is possible to say that Zen has eaten its way into the depths of modern-day Japanese people's lives through our traditional culture, which stems from Zen.

Since Zen was not something that could be seen, attempts were made to express it formally within the arts. Zen involves diligence and self-purification, and so priests made Zen gardens in order to study. We call this *ishidateso*, which literally means the placing of stones by a monk; and to understand the stones is to be able to read their heart, or *ishigokoro*. At this point I must explain the importance of stone in a Japanese garden, because it occupies a role not found in the West. Stones have a spiritual life as much as do plants and animals, and in the development of the Zen garden they became the most important element. For a priest designing a garden, the point is how to simplify, to best achieve the essence: not to continue adding but to use simple materials to express everything. Here, stone is the key.

The path to simplicity in a Zen garden, whether ancient or modern, is to express nature in a pure form, without plants and without water. This is how the dry-stone garden, or *karesansui*, developed. With sand and the different scales of stone it is possible to represent all of nature. It is also possible to express concepts through garden design, as in the Ryumontei, or Dragon Gate, garden at Gion-ji temple in Mito, shown opposite. This is a parable within an historical story, set in the seventeenth century in this area, where Buddhism was in decline, with many fake priests. The Vice-Shogun Mitomitsukuni invited

The act of raking the white sand into a pattern recalling waves or rippling water has an aesthetic function, but it is also an exercise that Zen priests practise to help them focus their concentration. Achieving perfection of line is not easy, and they make their own rakes according to the pattern of ridges desired.

When the screens of a traditional *tatami* room are fully pulled back, the garden is considered to flow into it. This blurring of the division between garden and house, exterior and interior, is deliberate, and is aided by the similar levels of floor and ground, and by the absence of a raised sill.

a famous priest from Nagasaki called Shinetsu to establish this temple, and this garden, which I made in 2000, shows the two of them. On the left, the Vice-Shogun and an audience are ranged in front of the priest, who tells them the tale illustrated by the stones on the right – a parable from China about the carp who struggles upriver to surmount the rapids that pour through the Dragon Gate. This is a metaphor for struggle in overcoming adversity, and ultimately a metaphor for self-enlightenment.

I mention this as an example of how the garden in Japan can express so much. There are other methods besides dry stone, many surprisingly modern in their conceptual purity. I have already mentioned simplicity and the reduction of the garden to the essential, and touched upon how we can focus on a single element, making more of less, rather than the all-too-common less out of more. Other highly developed techniques are viewpoint and composition, which involve a measure of control, directing the experience that a person will have of the garden. This can take the form of trimming the view, of revealing some but not all, of presenting different views from different positions, sometimes in sequence, sometimes as alternatives. One of the most striking techniques is the borrowed view, or *shakkei*, in which part of a distant landscape is "captured" and brought into the artist's rendering of the garden. This is increasingly difficult to achieve because of Japan's overcrowding, but you can see it at work in my Canadian Embassy garden (see pages 82–5), and in an unusual way in the Asian Gate house in Okinawa (see pages 34–9).

There are different aesthetics and many expressions, but behind each of the gardens in this book, which represent the contemporary scene in gardening, there is an idea, a philosophy. The gardens address new concerns relating to modern living and space, and they sometimes use new materials, but their designers are, in most cases, using established techniques from our rich Japanese repertoire.

What are the new trends in Japanese gardens? My own preoccupation, naturally, is with the application of Zen, through garden design, to modern life, meaning in particular urban life. By using stone and metaphor I try to create gardens that summon one to a simpler way of viewing the world. More generally, I can see Japanese gardeners and architects responding to the changing needs of people in our society.

The density of urban housing and the lack of private space are special modern problems. In some ways, I'm afraid, we Japanese lead the world in this respect, which places on us a responsibility to deal with it spiritually, and that for me is the key role of a garden. Fortunately, our long experience with closely packed housing and limited space has equipped us well to devise strategies for managing that space to its best advantage. There has long been an ideal in the Japanese house of integrating the garden with the building. You can see this traditionally in the way translucent *shoji* screens are used, and can be opened right up. In more restricted modern spaces there are other ways of achieving this, as in the tiny vertical houses designed by Denso Sugiura (see pages 64–7).

New materials and new ways of treating materials widen our scope. For example, I am especially interested in the uses of hewn stone – a radical break from the old

Open to the sky, in the centre of Japan's famous
traditional Tawaraya Inn, is a typical small courtyard
garden, or *tsubo-niwa*. A corridor opens fully onto
both sides of this area, where the key elements are
a surface of pebbles, a flat stone for the traditional
clogs, or *geta*, and a stone water basin with its ladle.

❯
Stone has always been of great importance in Japanese garden design, and a major innovation of recent years is the use of hewn stone such as this.

❮
With a long history to draw on, modern Japanese garden design usually makes reference to earlier principles. To create this sunken garden in the Osaka suburb of Sakuragaoka, architect Osamu Ishii excavated the plot to a depth of 4m (13ft) below the ground. The square pond is non-traditional, but its shape, with crossed corners, is known as *igeta*, a design element found in several contexts, from textiles to the floats carried in religious processions.

tradition of using stones only as they are found in nature. Split edges and rows of wedging grooves reveal a different kind of beauty in stone. Other designers have found uses for glass, iron, stainless steel, tiles, and even carbon fibre, as a number of the gardens shown in this book illustrate.

Then there is the choice of elements – principally the plants and stones. In the 1950s Kiyoshi Seike was one of the first garden designers to introduce a freer style of planting, and today we can see even more of this freedom: the use of the semi-wild – for example, imported plants – and the re-creation of specific habitats, such as the broadleaf evergreen plants of a Shinto shrine.

I hope that from these examples you may draw some inspiration for your own garden space. The environment, the people who will use the garden, and the relationship of the garden with the building – these are the first priorities to consider, and only after this can the designer begin. This principle applies to anyone who would like to create their own garden.

If the scenery surrounding your home is beautiful, why not create a garden that continues towards this view, as in the Sekkasanbo house (see pages 72–5)? That will help make the garden feel much bigger than its actual size, and make it comfortable. On the other hand, if you don't like the noise and the view where your home is situated, why not make a wall to exclude them, and create a nice, quiet *tsubo* garden, as in the "Residence the Colour of Ink" (see pages 26–9)? If your work is hard, you might consider creating a space in front of the entrance, where you can "tune up" – a tiny *genkan* garden, perhaps with a tree and stepping stones (see pages 86–7). When size is the problem, as it so often is, then again the wisdom of the Japanese garden can help, in applying "ambiguity of space." As a small example, see how the placing of plants near a window can be made to suggest a continuous scene with bushes and trees in a garden, and so create an open atmosphere (see pages 56–9).

It is very easy for people who lead urban lives, with the accompanying strain of work, to lose sight of their own identity. The importance of the garden is the way in which it can help to remedy this. A space that embodies nature can act as a kind of balm – a restorative for the mind. In its ideal form, the modern Japanese garden is just that spiritual space, designed according to a sophisticated aesthetic that evokes and celebrates nature. The means used differ, as we can see throughout this book, from Zen dry stone to the focus on a single tree, to freer, wilder forms of planting, but all draw on a thousand years of what we call *tokikata* – in this context, the reading of the cosmos through the garden. Ultimately, this is how I see the modern garden in Japan – a space that provides the means for the mind to become acutely sensitive to the simple, small matters that are often blanketed by daily life.

⟩
This unusual wooden structure, part free-standing wall, part arch, has the function of restricting the view of the stone garden from the entrance to the house. The idea is to reveal just enough to intrigue the visitor. The inspiration for the opening is the low "wriggling-in entrance" to a tea-ceremony room.

☾
Traditional dry-stone gardens have one formally framed view – usually from inside a temple. Here the view is from the ground floor, but the floor is on the same level as the garden instead of being raised.

contemporary dry stone
design: yoshiji takehara

The dry-stone garden, or *karesansui*, as exemplified by Shunmyo Masuno's contemporary but traditionally correct design at Gion-ji temple in Mito (see page 10), is inextricable from Zen Buddhism. Yet, as Masuno writes, its appreciation has spread into secular culture, and it has a great appeal for many Japanese in the setting of the home. In this garden on the slopes of Hieizan, a sacred mountain close to Kyoto, architect Yoshiji Takehara made a modern dry-stone garden a central feature of the house. Both house and garden were completed in 2001 for the client, who is a textile artist.

The inspiration for this *karesansui* was the fact that the owner's father had collected attractive stones for many years. Each one was significant, and had a name and a history. When the time came to rebuild the site, Takehara realized that the arrangement and the relationship of the principal stones should be preserved. However, he removed the trees and most of the other plantings, and looked for a way to enhance the siting of the stones and give the garden coherence. He recommended relying on the purity of stone, which would mean turning a fairly standard garden into a *karesansui*. Normally the base surface in a dry-stone garden is white sand, representing water, but Takehara modernized this element by using *warikuri-ishi*, broken stone. This would have an even drier appearance than sand, and permitted the use of different sizes for a more dynamic representation of flowing water, as in Masuno's courtyard garden in Kojimachi (see pages 76–81).

House and garden work together to give interesting views, and exploit the concept of *tachidomaru*. This word is a combination of "stand" and "stop" and means "to pause, stop, and look back." One feature found in temples – and Takehara draws attention in particular to the Daitoku temple in Kyoto – is that the route that has to be taken to reach one part or another is always circuitous, with twists and turns, so that progress towards the destination always contains the unexpected. The experience of walking from point A to point B gives the visitor different views. "What you first saw and expected as the scene that would greet you is changed through views that reveal themselves as you progress along the route, and this traditional method of design is what I try to incorporate in my residential houses," explains Takehara.

An essential part of this unexpectedness is to give glimpses and partial or blocked-off views, so as to intrigue the visitor. These may or may not be resolved by further views from within the house, but the uncertainty and ambiguity are important to Takehara in order to establish interest. (He achieves this in a different way by creating interconnected spaces in the garden on pages 56–9.) Here, he wanted to control the immediate view from the street entrance. The short path leads to the front door, in a wing of the house that contains a modernized *tatami* room, or *washitsu*, a room floored with mats of reinforced rush. Left alone, this layout would reveal a side view of the dry-stone garden, and Takehara wanted to avoid such an immediate exposure. At the same time, however, he did not want to hide it completely, but rather to let the visitor know that something interesting is about to happen.

His solution was to construct a massive, free-standing wooden arch – a thick wall with a low rectangular opening. Structurally this is ambiguous, and seems to have no function. In fact, its purpose is to encourage the visitor to walk over and crouch down to see what is on the other side. Indeed the size and positioning of the opening intentionally resembles the "wriggling-in entrance" of a tea-ceremony room. In setting it 1m (3ft) in front of the *tatami* room, Takehara simultaneously added a small passageway, which offers another invitation to walk down and see what there is. "To make various things happen as people walk between houses is an essential part of my architecture," he says.

Eventually the visitor is rewarded with two complete views of the dry-stone garden. The first is from the ground floor, where a raised *tatami* floor gives a perfectly framed view. Here Takehara insisted on keeping the level of the lower concrete floor at exactly that of the garden (conventionally it would be higher), in a deliberate move to confuse interior and exterior. In the upper-floor dining area, screens can be slid back to reveal a view from above.

Immediately to the left of the front door of the house is a small *tatami* room for use by guests and for the display of the owner's textile designs. A floor-to-ceiling screen in the far wall slides back to give a view through a wooden arch. The concrete wall on the left was cast with wooden planks, to echo the texture of the wood used for the arch.

The architect's design makes maximum use of different views across spaces. As one leaves the view on the left and rounds the corner, the arrangement of openings and geometric planes on the other side of the *tatami* room gives a different framing of a few key stones in the garden beyond.

The view from the upper floor looks down onto the
garden and includes a balcony lined with flowerpots.
Traditional dry-stone gardens do not have such an
overhead view.

bringing the garden into the house

design: suiko nagakura

One of the outstanding features of traditional Japanese housing is the integration of house and garden. Indeed the word for garden, *niwa*, when written in the archaic form, uses the characters that mean "house front." The use of paper *shoji* screens, which slide back to open the interior up completely to the exterior, with a veranda as a connecting space that is neither inside nor outside, plays an essential role in this.

Here, in the house of potter Suiko Nagakura, the idea appears to have been taken to an extreme, for the dining room is the garden, and a fairly wild one at that, with ferns growing around the legs of the table. The fecundity of the room is not surprising, given that the floor is earth, which the owner keeps well watered, adding to its nourishment by throwing onto it the remains of the occasional cup of green tea. This interior garden extends down another side of the house as a kind of inside-outside corridor, while the conventional living areas, floored with *tatami*, are on a raised platform, partly enclosed by the L-shape of earth and greenery. The exterior walls that enclose the garden are plastered wood, with full-height sliding windows along the south-facing corridor, allowing plenty of light for the pink and red geraniums growing there. All of this particularly suits the owner's dog, Lily.

If one considers the Japanese architectural tradition, the idea of bringing the garden into the house is not actually as strange as it may at first seem to a Westerner. The earth floor is a direct descendant of the *doma* – an interior space with a floor of packed earth that has almost completely disappeared from Japanese houses. The *doma* was a workspace, a traffic space, and a location for the kitchen, while the proper floor was raised. Indeed, at the entrance to almost every Japanese house today, the lobby area where shoes are removed is a step below the main level, and is still called the *doma*.

Packed earth has long been a feature of Japanese houses, but it was restricted to the area immediately surrounding the raised floor, and never used for normal rooms, such as this modern dining room, except in the poorest homes.

Before the house was built in 1995, the land was a field of barley and tobacco. "Maybe that is why things seem to grow easily here," says Nagakura. "Sometimes there is barley, sometimes dandelions, without my having to do anything. Last winter a frog came in to hibernate." At first she had not thought of creating a garden, but just wanted to have the convenience of a *doma*. Gradually, however, plants began to invade, such as the curled mallow (*Malva verticillata*), a famous symbol for the Tokugawa shogunate, and she enjoyed the effect so much that she started to add her own plants, including the medicinal aloe, with its thick, sword-like leaves, bamboo palm, and Japanese hydrangea (*Hydrangea macrophylla*). She found that the natural style of her ceramics blended well with the ferns and other plants, so she set a number of pieces strategically around the room, including under one side of the dining table, as focal points. The room now doubles as a showroom for her work. In addition to arranging temporary exhibits around the room, she has permanently embedded others in the garden among the plants.

The slight element of natural chaos, or at least the unplanned progress of nature, is in accord with Nagakura's own ceramic works. "What I like about this garden is that it obeys no man-made rules – just like clay. Both are elements of nature, and I do not want to impose any artificiality on it." One of her techniques with clay is to introduce random effects: at a certain stage in the modelling she closes her eyes and squeezes or hits it. In an analogous way she welcomes the accident of wild species taking hold in the dining-room garden. Pointing to the maidenhair fern (*Adiantum capillus-veneris*) growing beneath the table, she says, "When it first established itself it was over there, a little more to the north, but day by day it has been moving round to the south."

◗

The view from the side of the house near the rear reveals the relationship between house and garden. The living room, floored with *tatami* mats, is raised at the left, so that the garden runs around it. Sliding screens can be opened completely, allowing the owner to enjoy a full view of the interior garden.

◖

As the first room to be entered from the front door, the dining room doubles as a space in which to show off the owner's ceramics, which have an organic quality that matches the invading garden. Some pieces are temporarily displayed on shelves and on the table (right), while others are embedded in the garden (far right), where they act as an anchor for plants. Their presence helps to blur the distinction between the man-made and the natural.

The designer's solution to the problem of subdued light in this small courtyard enclosed by a three-storey house is to prepare the eye by making the front part of the ground floor dark.

urban courtyard
design: michimasa kawaguchi

The courtyard house originated in China, and from it came the courtyard garden, but in Japan there occurred the miniaturization that is an important aspect of its culture. Indeed the Japanese term for a courtyard garden, *tsubo niwa*, acknowledges this development by exaggeration. A *tsubo* is a traditional unit of area, the equivalent of two *tatami* mats laid out side by side, and measures 3.305 square metres (36 square feet). Most interior gardens in Japan are rather larger than this, but the term has stuck.

In this house in the residential suburb of Tokyo called Ichikawa, a courtyard garden was the logical solution to the problem of the property's location in a busy, noisy, and very built-up area. The space is organized lengthwise across a very slim, tapering block, with two narrow streets at the front and back. Unfortunately, both streets lead into a main thoroughfare just a few metres away, so that the house is almost surrounded by constant traffic. In fact, it is a familiar Japanese urban setting, and one that encouraged the architect, Michimasa Kawaguchi, to create an inward-looking house. The number of outside windows was reduced to a minimum, and the central garden, which can be viewed from both floors, was made the focus of attention.

Given this design, the available light is not generous, and the predictable solution would have been to maximize it by reflection, with white walls. But Kawaguchi was concerned that making the courtyard walls as bright as possible so as to deliver light into the ground-floor rooms would work to the detriment of the garden view. The view from the house onto the garden would have had too much contrast for comfort. His answer was to place the living room, dining room, and kitchen on the floor above, where they would receive more light, and to use grey for the courtyard walls. In this way, the experience of entering the house is, first, an immersion in darkness, which then gives way to a restful view of the muted garden. A corridor with large windows runs around the garden on two sides, and because the interior surfaces – walls, wooden columns and beams, and the

A tiny space at the rear of the house, in one corner, has been turned into a miniature garden just for viewing. This window opens onto the traditional *tatami* room, while a second window, round the corner to the right, gives a different view from the master bedroom.

In this plan of the ground floor, the courtyard is in the centre, and the tiny corner garden is to the lower left. The front door is in the top right, so that for anyone entering the house, the first window to be seen is the one shown in the photograph opposite.

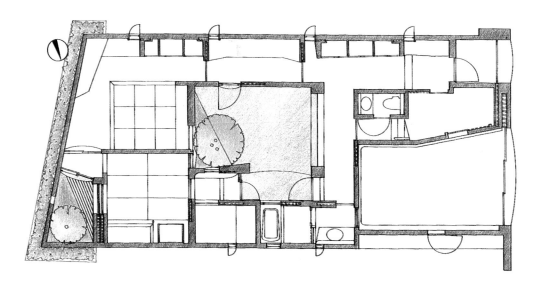

frames for *shoji* screens – are painted black and dark grey, there are no reflections in the glass when one looks out into the courtyard. On the floor above, there is more light, as well as a different perspective of the garden.

The varying shades of black and grey are carefully chosen, and are those of *sumi*, the ink used in calligraphy and for scroll paintings. Kawaguchi has used this ink in houses before for its natural quality, and for most Japanese it is both instantly recognizable and has pleasant cultural connotations. The finish is matt, and the wooden surfaces will, over time, acquire a natural sheen as they are repeatedly touched. One of the important qualities in the calligraphic and painting use of *sumi*, which comes in the form of ink stones and is applied by brush, is control over its tone. The amount of dilution is critical, and the shade of grey used for the courtyard walls – *usuzumi*, or "weak," *sumi* – is exact. The name of the house is Sumiiro no Jutaku, which means "Residence the Colour of Ink."

The owner is especially fond of potted plants, so only one side of the garden is planted, with a camellia, sacred or heavenly bamboo (*Nandina domestica*), and an aspidistra (*Aspidistra elatior*). Among the potted plants are a wax tree (*Rhus succedanea*) and a winter daphne (*Chloranthus glaber* 'Makino'). The *tatami* room is at the rear of the house, and Kawaguchi felt that it was essential for this to have its own contemplative garden view, however small. He arranged for a tiny, trapezoidal space to be left open in the acute angle of one corner of the property – space that would otherwise have been wasted – right up against the street wall. Light filters in here from above and reflects off the white-rendered walls. Measuring 2.5 square metres (27 square feet), this area is too small to enter except for maintenance, but two windows, one opening onto the *tatami* room, the other onto the adjacent main bedroom, give two different views of a Japanese quince (*Chaenomeles speciosa* 'Nakai'), with an aspidistra beneath it.

❯
Black pebbles, or *nach-ishi*, and ground cover surround the base of a camellia tree; the grass-like plant is the mat-forming evergreen perennial *Ophiopogon japonicus* (far left). Similar restraint in the use of colour is seen in culms of bamboo set against the grey wall at the front of the house (left).

A view of the courtyard from the first floor. The
palette of *usuzumi* (weak-ink) tones is matched
with plants in muted greens. Restraint in the use
of colour is one of the most traditional of Japanese
aesthetic principles.

While a major function of this sunken courtyard is to feed light into the rooms to the left and right, it is a striking space in its own right. Half its height is below ground level, and there are translucent windows on each side and a transparent wall at the end. The space is treated as a huge display case, dedicated to a single flowering dogwood (*Cornus florida*).

Two young trimmed Hioki cypress (*Chamaecyparis obtusa*) flank the front door. At this stage these popular trees are called *asunaro* – literally, "tomorrow to be." The horizontal lines of the corrugated-steel façade exaggerate the illusion of a long, low building when seen from the street, adding to the surprise of the deep sunken courtyard garden inside.

light well
design: **kazuyo sejima and ryue nishizawa**

A very different kind of courtyard garden from Michimasa Kawaguchi's in Ichikawa (see pages 26–9) solved a similar problem of privacy in the M-House, which was designed by the architectural team of Kazuyo Sejima and Ryue Nishizawa for a client who works in the music industry. The property is also located in Tokyo, in the exclusive residential district of Shibuya. Over the years the plots have gradually been subdivided, so that nowadays the average area is some 200 square metres (2,150 square feet), which, by Japanese standards, is very generous. Nevertheless, the houses themselves are generally large, filling the spaces, so that even in this desirable part of the city there is still a sense of overcrowding. Many houses are Western in style, and have windows that look out onto the street and other properties. This proximity has led most occupants to fit blinds or curtains, which are usually closed.

Sejima and Nishizawa immediately recognized these "anomalies," as they describe them, and looked for a way in this house to "bring the outside into the interior while at the same time securing privacy for the living space." Specifically, the owner also wanted an area for parties. "Our solution," the architects continue, "was to dig up the entire site." By excavating below ground level and creating a central garden court, they were able to place the main living areas attractively at this lower level, keeping the parts of the dwelling that were not communal (garage, bedrooms, and guest room) at street level.

"Basements are generally rated low in livability, but, by arranging very open areas around a light court, we made the entire basement a pleasant space filled with air and light. A large space that is continuous both visually and experientially was created." The central light well that contains the garden measures 10m (33ft) by nearly 3m (10ft), and is slightly more than 5m (16ft) deep. Most of the light enters from above, filtered by white-painted steel louvres, and additional light comes from a double screen of perforated metal

at one end at street level. The perforations are small enough to maintain privacy. Floor-to-ceiling partitions made of translucent polycarbonate and glass line both of the long sides, passing light through to the living room on one side and the studio on the other, while also helping to keep the court itself bright and light. At one end is a white concrete wall, while at the other a passage with a full glass wall gives a view of the court to people walking between the two halves of the house. The depth and spacing of the louvres is carefully designed to allow maximum natural light from above, while hiding surrounding buildings.

After consultation with the architects the owners chose to keep the garden a model of simplicity, in which all attention focused on a single tree growing through a square opening in the wooden decking. They chose a flowering dogwood (*Cornus florida*), imported from the United States; this rises the full height of the light well, and flowers in late spring. The height, slim trunk, and delicacy of this species have recently made it popular in Japan's parks and private gardens, illustrating how taste has moved away from the hard, sculptural style of trimmed conifers towards a more natural, softer appearance. Here the flowering dogwood occupies an almost iconic position at the far end of the court from the main door leading from the living room, doubly reflected in the glass and polycarbonate walls and softening the pattern of vertical and horizontal lines.

Oddly, the M-House was included in the well-publicized 1999 show "The Un-Private House" at New York's Museum of Modern Art – an interesting example of how easily misunderstood are some of the principles of Japanese architecture and garden design. Far from being "un-private," the creation of Sejima and Nishizawa provided a precise answer to their clients' request for privacy.

White-painted steel louvres span the opening of the light well. They admit light but restrict views of the courtyard from neighbouring houses. In sunlight they also add a linear pattern to the scene.

Seen here in the evening, with the glow from the interior lights seeping through the translucent walls, the dogwood's delicate outline contrasts gently with the minimalist lines and planes of the box-like light well.

The light well divides the house – the living room is on the left, the study and upstairs bedrooms on the right – but a narrow corridor (not shown on the plan) runs across the upper end, behind the dogwood.

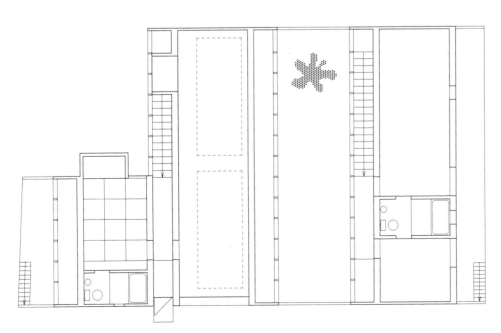

In this shallow bay the tide ebbs a long way, changing the view, which is "borrowed" by framing it with a symmetry to which the palm trees contribute. The rock is visually enclosed by the shape of the deck.

modern shakkei
design: tetsuo goto and amon miyamoto

One of the boldest techniques in the tradition of the Japanese garden is *shakkei*, or "borrowed view," In principle it is straightforward – a distant natural feature of the landscape is used to complete the design of a garden – but in practice it demands not only an extremely careful choice of site, but also a refined sense of composition. Teiji Itoh, in his book *Space and Illusion in the Japanese Garden* (1973), traces the origins of *shakkei* to seventh-century China, but it developed separately in Japan, where the original term for it was *ikedori*, meaning "to capture alive."

There are a number of implications inherent in the idea of *shakkei*. One is that there should be sufficient expansive landscape in the surroundings to offer the possibility of creating it. Another is that the distant element, which is out of the gardener's control, will not change substantially. A third is that the view, and therefore the exact position of the viewer in relation to the garden, should be precisely controlled. This last element is a recurring feature in much Japanese gardening and is linked to the idea of framing views from interiors by means of screens and verandas.

Of these three requirements, only the last can still be fully realized, and in this Okinawan seaside house, called Asian Gate, extraordinary use has been made of it. As for the other two, the modern Japanese landscape is less and less amenable to *shakkei* as high-rise buildings sprout, and power lines march across the hills. Indeed, there is no guarantee that what was originally a carefully planned view may not be ruined, as a recent instance in Kyoto highlighted (see pages 42–5). The most carefully laid plans are always at risk, owing to the modern problem of borrowing rather than owning a landscape.

Architect Tetsuo Goto and owner Amon Miyamoto devised a highly imaginative and original solution. Miyamoto, a well-known theatre and film director, had fallen in love with the southern Japanese island of Okinawa, and bought a seafront plot of land overlooking a rocky bay. Traditional Okinawan houses are set back from the shore because of the annual typhoon season, but Miyamoto chose this site at the edge of a low cliff for its view. This part of the island is known for its isolated wave-cut limestone rocks – undercutting of the soft stone creates some dramatic shapes – and one of them lay directly opposite the site, perched on the flat, seaweed-draped rock bed of the bay. The planes of the rock bed are so flat, in fact, that the tide recedes almost to the distant headland.

This was the inspiration for a modern *shakkei* that is borrowed seascape more than borrowed landscape. Unlike the traditional form, it embraces change – for while distant hills alter only slowly with the seasons, this view is in a constant flux, which is noticeable by the hour. At high tide only the "captured" rock breaks the expanse of blue water, while at low tide the view is of almost completely dry land, green with seaweed. Add to this the procession of the tides, and the seasonal variations in their height and in the position of the sun, and the view from Asian Gate never remains exactly the same.

Okinawa is the southernmost part of Japan, and its almost tropical climate supports a distinctive flora, including bougainvillea. This gnarled specimen close to the small reflecting pool has embedded its roots in the weathered limestone that provides this coastline with its characteristic free-standing rocks.

◡

An early sketch shows that the architect and owner agreed that the rock's upper part should fit visually into an indentation when seen from the house. This was later achieved with decking that embraces the rock.

☾

Reflecting pools have a long history in Japanese gardening. Here the reflection gives the illusory impression that there is a continuity between the water in the pool and the sea.

To "capture" the rock and bay, Goto carefully aligned the central section of the concrete house (built into the slope for protection from typhoons) and extended the large living area seamlessly by means of a wide, rectangular opening that gives onto a wooden deck. Two wings of the deck enclose the rock visually, while *tokkuriyashi* palm trees (a type of bottle palm named for its shape, which is similar to that of a saké decanter), project through holes on each side, enhancing the symmetry of the view. The unusual shape of the large rock, some 5m (16ft) tall, contributes to the illusion that is at the heart of *shakkei*. As there is no reference for scale, it could be any size, and from the viewing position at the low table that dominates the living room the visitor does not even have the benefit of parallax to give a clue. Only by standing up and walking out to the veranda can you understand the illusion – and it always comes as a surprise when first seen.

Not content with capturing the rock and bay from the living room, Goto and Miyamoto went on to find other *shakkei* uses for them. On the left side of the house a covered walkway leads down to a small reflecting pool that mirrors the sky and blends with the view of the water in the bay. On the right side they created a *tour de force* in the tea-ceremony room. According to Miyamoto, "I studied the tea ceremony as a child, but I had a simple and innocent idea – I wanted a window, to see everything." This runs counter to one of the expressions of the Japanese tea ceremony, which is restriction of view, but here in his Okinawan house Miyamoto had the opportunity to realize it. The focus of such rooms is the *tokonoma*, an alcove for the display of objects of symbolic importance. Typically, a *kakejiku*, or scroll painting, is hung there, and usually this features a natural landscape. The stroke of brilliance here was to imitate a scroll-painting landscape with the real one, by cutting a narrow window looking out towards the bay. And, as in a scroll painting, the composition discloses just a part of the rock such as a mountain slope. Below the window, the traditional flower container is replaced by a shallow depression in a red-lacquered ledge, as a single orchid bloom floats in the tiny pool.

Thus the rock plays a key role in the life of the house. Miyamoto senses its spirit, and the choice and positioning of the two palm trees deliberately suggest a shrine. With his love of theatre and dance, he sometimes stages performances on the terrace. "In particular," he says, "the music of the *kokyu* [a guitar-like Chinese instrument] blends with the sound of the waves swelling round the rock." The Asian Gate's "borrowed" view is garden, shrine, and stage.

In an impressive modern interpretation of a tea-ceremony room, the traditional landscape scroll painting – a primary influence on Japanese garden design – is imaginatively replaced by a real view. The way in which the rock is cropped, so that just one edge is revealed, deliberately mimics a mountainside as it would be depicted in such a painting.

A circular depression in the red-lacquered ledge in the tea-ceremony room serves as a miniature pool for a floating orchid flower. The curve of the polished ledge and the meniscus of the water reflect the light that enters through the single, tall, vertical window.

lightening the path
design: shuji mizudome

This house in Saitama prefecture includes a tea-ceremony room, or *chashitsu*, to the left of the entrance, and, in keeping with Japanese practice, certain elements are required in the garden that leads to it. Traditionally, these can be quite demanding, as in Kisho Kurokawa's garden on an apartment terrace (see pages 50–3), and, to be strictly correct, they should include a path of stepping stones, a stone water basin for ritual cleansing, a stone lantern, and more. But here there was insufficient room, and, besides, the owner wanted a lighter, more modern approach. She approached artist Shuji Mizudome to find a solution that would not break with tradition, but rather evolve it – all in a small space.

Mizudome combines garden design with his other creative work in installation and video art, and at the same time as choosing plants that would make the garden more lively, he focused his attention on the path. Stepping stones across a sea of gravel or sand are traditional, but these are too heavy in appearance for those who, like the client, have grown up under the influence of Western and modern Japanese design. Mizudome decided to make a path that evolves as it progresses from tea house to gate, from "heavy" tradition to light modern, and in this way symbolizes the evolution of Japanese culture.

One of the most important stones in the path leading to a tea-ceremony room is the large one just in front of the sliding door. This spans the *tataki* (a sill that runs around the house) and the gravel, and is known as the *kutsunugi-ishi* – literally, the stone where shoes are removed. For this stone, Mizudome stuck firmly to tradition by selecting a kind of granite known as *kurama-ishi*, characterized by its brown colour, which comes from a high iron content, and a flaking appearance. Marking a move away from tradition, the next two stones are quite ordinary – they came from a regular garden supply shop – and these lead to this Mizudome's own creation.

This consists of a special cement mixture, set with small rocks and green pebbles – a composition created by Mizudome with great care. He was concerned not just with texture but with colour and tone, and, to his artist's eye, regular cement would be too bright. By experiment he arrived at a mixture that included a powder from a weathered granite called *masago*, and this proved to be sufficiently muted. Into this he set a pattern of brown granite stones with a softer appearance than the forceful *kurama-ishi* at the entrance to the tea-ceremony room, and curving patterns of green, river-washed pebbles from Ryokkaseki, inserted end-on. In his design the pebbles represent music. He maintained these two kinds of stone at an even level above the cement by setting them deep, flush with the surface of the cement, and then, when this had half dried, washing it with water.

Before Mizudome began work, the garden already contained a fifty-year-old Japanese maple (*Acer palmatum*) that was a favourite of the owner, and to this he principally added deciduous trees, and a few evergreens for variety. A small, south-facing garden such as this needs mainly deciduous trees to give maximum light in the winter and yet provide shade in Japan's hot summers. One tree Mizudome chose is a full-moon maple (*Acer japonicum*), with a light blue-grey bark and large leaves. Another is a rowan or mountain ash (*Sorbus aucuparia*), which gives white flowers in summer.

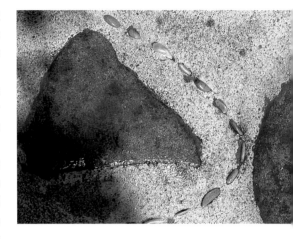

Smooth, green pebbles, embedded in cement to form curves and parabolas that run around the larger granite stones, add interest to the pattern. For the designer of the garden they symbolize musical notes.

The sequence of stepping stones that leads from the gate (out of view to the left) to the tea-ceremony room, here sheltered by *shoji* screens, is the key feature of this small garden. Mizudome has used three contrasting types of stone: a single traditional and expensive one closest to the room, seen here lit by the sun; two relatively ordinary stones in front of it; and, in the foreground, his own composition – brown granite stones and green pebbles set in a cement that he devised for the purpose.

The garden is designed to be experienced dynamically, and this process begins with the approach from the small door leading off the porch. Even this initial view is rigorously composed. The pattern of the rectangular slabs that form the path is a deliberate counterpoint to the frame created by the walls and roof overhang beyond, while the tree on the right neatly fills the right-hand part of this frame.

Because the property combines two plots on different levels, the designer was able to make full use of the slope between them to create a scene that fills the view obtained from the living room. The composition is organized vertically, from the rock-and-tile rainwater trough immediately in front of the room, through a broad band of moss, to the large stone, and finally the wall of the owner's studio.

a preparation for painting
design: atsushi akenuki

Kyoto-based garden designer Atsushi Akenuki is an unassuming man with a considerable reputation. He was chosen by the architect I.M. Pei to design the garden for the 1996 Miho Museum in Shiga prefecture, while locally he is in charge of the garden of Japan's best-known *ryokan*, or traditional inn, the Tawaraya. Kyoto regards itself, with some justification, as the fountain of Japanese culture, an attitude that breeds some resentment in other parts of the country. Nevertheless, this is where the arts have flourished more prominently than elsewhere in Japan. The city has the greatest concentration of great temple gardens, including the most famous of all, Ryoan-ji, which dates from 1488, and, even at the secular level, people here take their gardens very seriously.

So seriously, in fact, that when in 2000 a neighbour of the famous Tawaraya Inn decided to build a high-rise apartment block right next door, it caused local uproar and made the international news. For the Tawaraya's calm and delightful garden, onto which the guest rooms opened, this was rather the reverse of *shakkei*, the "borrowed view" (see pages 34–9), for here the view was being robbed, and worse still, the new tenants would be able to see into the renowned and expensive accommodation. This problem had to be solved by Akenuki. "I planted some tall trees," he says laconically.

Another of Kyoto's institutions is the painter Akira Kaho (winner of the 1982 Japan Art Prize, the Nihon Geijutsu Taisho), and for his house he asked Akenuki to design a garden that would assist his work. Kaho argues for a reappraisal of what Japan's traditions – too rigid and top-heavy for some – can teach us. No lover of Post-Modernism, which he sees as mannered, or of Modernism for that matter, he prefers to extract some of the fundamentals of Japanese art, including that of the garden, to provide modern inspiration.

The owner's most treasured item in the garden is this uniquely textured, flat-topped stone, seen here from the entrance to the studio. As its purpose is inspirational, the stone had to be positioned here, directly opposite the studio, but this required the demolition and rebuilding of the entire wall behind it.

Miniature gullies course the surface of the stone, created by differential erosion, and account for its considerable rarity and great expense. In Tottori prefecture, the only place in Japan where this kind of stone occurs naturally, local legend has it that a mythical insect eats into the surface.

At the far end of the upper garden stands an irregularly shaped *tsukubai*, a water basin traditionally used for symbolic washing of the hands and face before the tea ceremony. A covering of moss as seen here takes many years to grow, and is highly prized for the character and sense of age that it gives to a garden.

Kaho's house extends over two former properties, at different levels, and he wanted to keep his studio separate from the living areas, to enable maximum concentration on his painting. In addition, he had the idea of using the garden to give access to the studio, so that the short outside walk would serve to prepare him for the day's work. It would do duty in the manner of a tea garden – an example of which Kisho Kurokawa has created in central Tokyo (see pages 50–3) – which prepares guests spiritually for the tea ceremony

Given the configuration of the site, in which the space available for the garden is on a short, steep slope, Akenuki saw the opportunity for two garden "experiences": One would be the walk to the studio – the "ritual of the passageway" – and the other a framed view from the living room. The framed view would have a special characteristic that would set it apart from normal treatments – it would be vertically arranged, and, with appropriate planting, need have no sky visible. As a painter, Kaho appreciated this frame-filling idea, but at the same time he had strong views about it. "In the sense that it is constantly changing, a garden is not the same as a painting. But at the same time, it should have the same pure honesty of a *sumi* – ink – painting. Sometimes a garden can speak too much. As in *sumi* painting, we should remove, not add, and so stimulate the imagination."

Sensitive to this, Akenuki laid out a garden of considerable subtlety within the frame of the window. A huge, dark, "table-top" stone keys the composition, while the ground, both in a painterly and a literal sense, is filled with hair-cap moss (*Polytrichum juniperinum*), which, at 10 cm (4in), grows tall for a moss, and has a thick, carpet-like texture. He planted three species of maple: mountain maple (*Acer matsumurae*), *Acer amoenum*, with leaves that are red all year, and Japanese maple (*Acer palmatum*), with leaves that turn brilliant yellow in autumn.

After the view from inside comes the walk to the studio, which takes the vistor through a covered passageway that frames the trees and steps beyond, and is followed by a different perspective of the sloping garden. Kaho likes to make the walk in traditional Japanese clogs, and Akenuki accommodated this wish by constructing a special *tataki, a* sill surrounding the house, that would be less noisy and more resilient than concrete. While researching ancient tumuli the architect found a mix of red earth, brine, and lime with which to make the *tataki*.

The final addition, which Kaho had been waiting twenty years to acquire, was a magnificent, unique black stone from Tottori prefecture. The differential erosion of this *sajiishi* stone has turned its flat top surface into a maze of deep runnels. Even for a stone-loving nation, this was an extravagant purchase, costing twenty million yen. "A stone like this is, for me, like a beautiful woman," Kaho says. "And now my friends say, "Well, you've finally got your geisha.""

a grove of carbon fibre

design: makato sei watanabe

Pillow-like ceramic casts from four subtly different moulds were laid in random combinations to give a half-organic, half-technological surface to the undulating garden. The carbon-fibre rods were then "planted" among these high-relief tiles.

The carbon-fibre rods are an advanced version of what was first installed in a garden in Gifu prefecture. Solar cells at the tips of the rods store energy during the day, and this is released at night as blue light by a recently developed form of diode.

As well as symbolizing the underworld of tubes and pipes that is the subject of the museum, the carbon-fibre rods also represent, according to Watanabe, "an interface connecting the solid, motionless building and the constantly changing nature – an etiquette of balance."

The development of Tokyo Bay was conceived as one of the great reclamation projects of modern urban planning. This was begun at the height of Japan's "bubble" economy, and its infrastructure was almost completed, and its superstructures about to go up, when the worst recession since the end of World War II hit the country in the early 1990s. What was to have been a huge new business district has been largely left on hold for a decade.

A basic infrastructural element that was in place before the bubble burst is the huge common tunnel system for pooling energy and information, and for waste disposal. The largest of its kind in Japan, it cost as much as a nuclear power plant to build. Architect Makato sei Watanabe was commissioned to design the K-Museum to put this system on public display. Land here has been reclaimed slowly since the early seventeenth century, when the village of Edo (now Tokyo) became the seat of the shogunal government, but what Watanabe calls the Tokyo "Frontier" is now a site rich in technology.

The fundamental issue facing Watanabe was what kind of work, and space, would be appropriate for this new "Frontier," an area, as he says, "devoid of any identity, with no older townscape to provide a point of reference, no cultural heritage to inherit, no nature to respect, and no future to forecast." He decided that the answer lay in light and movement. "This is reclamation land, once sea, and right down there at the foot of the steps leading up to the museum you can see and hear the waves lapping." The museum itself is a small but dynamic building composed of rectangular units that touch the ground only partially, with something of the appearance of a vehicle at "the moment of take off before flight or the moment of touchdown after a long flight," as the architect describes it.

To offset this angular dynamism, Watanabe decided to locate the building in a softer topography that would evoke both water and wind – the Bay's two most prominent natural features – yet using completely modern materials. The three-dimensional, curved floor of the undulating garden is covered with stone and tile. The stone is polished black granite, in closely fitting blocks, each with a complex curved surface. To achieve these three-dimensional granite shapes, Watanabe employed a computerized shaver to turn out three patterns, which, in the final, wave-like form, are assembled randomly. Surrounding the swelling black granite is a second undulating surface composed of small, pillow-like ceramic tiles, in four different mouldings, again assembled at random.

To bring life and a curious sense of nature to this assembly, the architect drew on an earlier experiment at Mura-no Terrace, in the countryside of Gifu prefecture. There he had "planted" a stand of tall, carbon-fibre rods adjacent to a grassy terrace, in allusion to the arrival of optical fibre and high-vision, large-screen televisions in the community, where, he says, "the people enjoy a comfortable life through the use of high technology within their beautiful natural surroundings." At the K-Museum the situation is different, since there is no beautiful nature on Tokyo Bay, but Watanabe found a new use for the thin, flexible rods, most of them around 3m (10ft) tall. "Touching the Wind" is a planting of "environmental sculptures" and the waves that the light-emitting rods make "are etched with slender silver lines that seem to whirl in the wind." Impressively, the strongly directional building seems to drift in a sea of black stone and tile, all seen through the kinetic waveforms of the grove of swaying rods.

city retreat
design: kisho kurokawa

In the Japanese gardening tradition, the opposite of *shakkei* – capturing a distant landscape for private use (see pages 34–9) – is the garden that leads to a tea-ceremony room. In this ceremony the approach to the tea room through a specially designed garden from which all exterior views are deliberately excluded plays a significant role in preparing guests by creating the right frame of mind. When Sen-no-Rikyu (1522–91) created the tea ceremony in the sixteenth century, he probably did not envisage such distracting surroundings as exist in modern metropolitan Japan. However, the idea of the *cha niwa* (*cha* means tea, *niwa* garden) is possibly even more relevant in such an environment. This was certainly the intention of the designer and owner of this pocket of contemplative calm perched high above the noise and activity of central Tokyo.

Kisho Kurokawa, one of the country's leading architects, whose works include the Hiroshima City Museum of Contemporary Art, created this antidote to an extremely busy location in the downtown Akasaka business and entertainment district, where he lives. The apartment, on the eleventh floor, is spacious, and also has a wide terrace. Whereas a typical Western solution might be to make full use of the openness of the terrace and create a party area, Kurokawa followed the tea-ceremony way. The apartment is in two sections: one is a modern living space, while the other, which contains the tea-ceremony room, is more traditional; two sections the terrace links them. The path to and through the garden leads from the living room, and is all the more effective in its progress because the immediate view from the sliding screens of the living room is startlingly urban, looking onto other high-rise blocks.

Just outside the door leading from the living room onto the terrace is a traditional large stepping stone, or *Kutsunugi-ishi*, and from here guests cross the open part of the terrace to a narrow path lined simply by a row of bamboo plants. This is the outer passageway, or *roji*, which makes a transition from the exterior to the tea garden itself. A simple gate opens

After leaving the modern section of the apartment and then crossing a path and stepping stones, the visitor reaches the entrance to the traditional rooms, which include one devoted to the tea ceremony. Looking out at the adjoining tea garden, the guest is presented with this scene of great peacefulness – a complete contrast to the view of the busy city offered by the other part of the dwelling.

Among the essential components of the tea garden is a *tsukubai*, or water basin for washing the hands and rinsing one's mouth. Guests use this in a symbolic act of purification that serves as a reminder of the Buddhist origins of the tea ceremony.

to reveal a compact, dense, and slightly disorienting garden, with pines and shrubs, traversed by natural stepping stones that lead over the earth and moss to a bed of gravel immediately in front of the tea-ceremony room, or inner *roji*. Among the shrubs is a stone *toro* lantern, present because tea ceremonies were sometimes held at night, and in front of this is a low stone water basin fed by a bamboo spout. This basin, the *tsukubai*, allowed guests to wash their hands and rinse their mouths in an act of symbolic cleansing. Such basins were low, compelling the guest to squat in front of it in an act of humility. Even this short distance contains the ritual of a passageway, of an approach to a special place.

In fact, although perched high over the city, this is a third-generation tea garden. It is a recreation of one in Kanunken, in the south of Kyoto, that was lost when the shrine of which it was a part, Iwashimizuhachimangu, was destroyed by fire in 1773. Even this, however, was not the original, for it in turn had been copied from another garden, known as Shosuitei, built by the famous tea master Enshu Kobori (1579–1647) for a residence in Kyoto. Reproducing Kobori's garden here, Kurokawa named this descendant Yuishikian.

Here, the greatest surprise comes on turning around at the entrance to the tea-ceremony room and looking back. All traces of the city disappear, hidden by the densely packed garden, which has been built up to a slightly higher level than the entrance. Kobori was the successor once removed to the great Sen-no-Rikyu as tea master to the Tokugawa shoguns, and he introduced a note of elegance to that master's aesthetic of poverty and restraint. In Kurokawa's garden, this quality is evident in the tight, controlled arrangement of trees and shrubs, some of which are trimmed and shaped.

In an old account of the teachings of the early tea masters, the garden is a natural realm of trees and rocks that signifies spiritual purity, removed from worldly defilement. Here, high above modern Tokyo at the start of the twenty-first century, this effect must be even more marked than it was in centuries past.

The garden, which occupies the corner of the property in the top-left area of the plan below, joins the two sections of the large apartment – the modern living area (top right) and the traditional rooms (bottom left). More practically, the two sections of the room are also linked by a corridor.

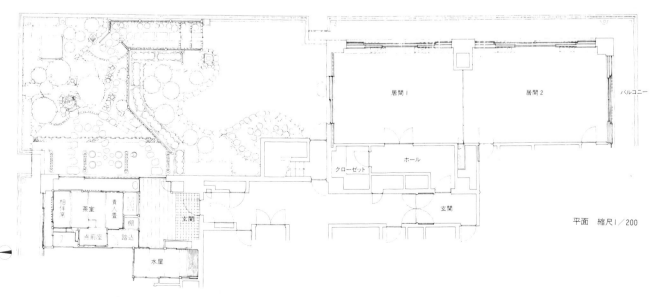

ambiguous spaces
design: yoshiji takehara

This large family house in a hilly residential suburb of Osaka stands on a steep slope, and architect Yoshiji Takehara has exploited this location by creating multiple levels, not only for accommodation, but also for the pleasure of circulating. The spaces between the many rooms make up the interconnected garden, and play an essential part in the design.

The Japanese word *ma* refers to spacing and timing, with particular relevance to the arts, and implies a subtle appreciation of the pause or gap. For example, in a Kabuki play the pause before an actor turns or speaks is known as *ma*; in calligraphy the amount of white space between the brushstrokes is decribed by the same term. This idea also plays a part in architecture, and is a preoccupation of Takehara, who says, "I am concerned with what we call *ma no kenchiku*, the architecture of ambiguous spaces."

The architect's interest in *ma* stems from the fact that in modern Japan the family unit is changing, especially the relationship between members and the way they interact on a day-to-day basis. These changes are the effect of factors in modern city life such as a falling birth rate, mobility, commuting, and reliance on convenience stores. "Families are becoming smaller and more fragmented," Takehara says, "and so I would like to make residences that are more collective in style." By "collective," he means that he is looking for an alternative to the typical single, subdivided interior space surrounded by its garden.

His solution, which depends to some extent on having a large enough area and several family members living together, is to use connecting courtyards and passageways as spaces, or *ma*, between rooms, "a kind of unit," he points out, "which was evident in former Japanese communities." Takehara believes that something has been lost in modern life – the kind of communication between people who regularly pass and meet each other as they move from one building to another – and he hopes that, by exploiting the ambiguity of small garden spaces, this kind of communal relationship can be revived.

For Takehara, this "ambiguity" begins at the street-level entrance to this house – a space between two walls of granite stones, assembled by the well-known stonemason Masatoshi Izumi. By placing large stones at the end of the outer wall and using considerably smaller ones for the inner wall, which lies 1m (3ft) behind it, Izumi and Takehara use

)
The street entrance, where the path makes a disconcerting right-angled turn, contains a deliberate illusion of perspective. The front wall is laid with larger stones than are used for the wall behind, so that the gap between the two – actually the width of a normal path – seems to be much larger than it really is.

(
Further turns, with views at each point, await the visitor. The path from the street goes through a dark passageway before emerging into a space that is part courtyard and part stairwell. Standing here are three concrete pillars, cast in forms lined with wood to symbolize tree trunks.

Reached only after following tortuous passageways, this modern tea-ceremony room is a calm, hidden space. With the screens open, the view is of a small garden, walled with concrete and planted with *mosodake* bamboo (*Phyllostachys pubescens*).

The growth of the *mosodake* bamboo is controlled by the use of a horizontal frame of cut bamboo, installed at head height. This encourages the young plant to rise in the ordered, vertical manner that characterizes its frequent use in the Japanese garden.

perspective of scale to give an illusion of depth. The open path becomes a short, dark passageway, which in turn opens out into a distinctly ambiguous space. This space is a courtyard of stone and concrete in a deep well, with a dogwood (*Cornus kousa*) in one corner by the main steps leading to the upper living level. In fact, from here it is possible to head in two opposite directions – left towards these steps, or right through a curious narrow alley that opens out, surprisingly, onto a courtyard of green bamboo.

On the level above, which is reached by the main steps, a series of walkways and terraces have a different, more open, sense of space. Some of these walkways give views down onto trees and plants, some of which are planted in unexpected corners. "By adding these small spaces and variety of routes, I am making the house a more comfortable place. At one turn a tree comes into view, at another a bed of stones, or a stand of bamboo," Takehara explains. Glimpses here and there of different plants and rocks keep the viewer's interest alive, while the number and variety of these small, related garden spaces make the residence feel more spacious than it really is.

This interconnectivity is one of the strongest features of the house, but Takehara has not neglected the static experience of being in one room. By carefully working out the lines of sight, he has given a green view from every window. The tea-ceremony room looks out onto a stand of bamboo, the kitchen and dining room have views down onto the same bamboo and simultaneously across to an ash tree (*Fraxinus japonica*), planted in its own tiny plot of earth set into a steep concrete slope, and so on. The garden may be divided in a seemingly random way, yet there is nowhere in this complex arrangement of interlocking spaces that lacks a touch of green.

The irregular layout of the upper levels of the house allows opportunities to create tiny spaces such as this exterior corner. These are filled with concrete slopes, each of which is planted with a tree. One slope contains this small ash, visible from the dining room.

The exterior planting scheme was conceived at the same time as the architectural plans, and integrated with the design of the house. Occupying a cut-away corner of the building is a Japanese stewartia (*Stewartia pseudocamellia*), while the corrugated-steel side wall is bordered with dwarf azalea. Both plants were chosen to soften the lines of the house.

The rooms on all three floors are set back slightly from the wall to leave a narrow light well, which is roofed by a pitched skylight that runs the length of the house. A stand of *mosodake* bamboo (*Phyllostachys pubescens*), seen here from the first landing, grows to the full height of the building.

vertically integrated bamboo
design: denso sugiura

Since 1995 Denso Sugiura has become well known for his unique solutions to one of Tokyo's most pressing needs – how to create houses on minuscule plots of land. Even by Japanese standards, the spaces he chooses to work with are restricted; with an average area of about 30 square metres (320 square feet), these would be adequate for a family garage in the United States. Although such plots are by no means unusual in Japan, the traditional approach results in something very far from a dream house. Sugiura's clients, however, tend to be either young professionals in media or advertising, or retired couples who want an attractive home in the city, and demand a more imaginative solution.

What Sugiura calls his *Chitchana* (Tiny Houses), of which fifteen have been built to date, share a number of common themes, but they are by no means formula dwellings. Verticality is the principal idea, but what has made the series so successful is the apparently generous allocation of space to a garden for each house. While he accepts that allowing space for non-utilitarian needs would be generous when it is at such a premium, Sugiura believes that "spending" some of this space on nature improves the quality of life inside the home. "When the Japanese economy was soaring, back in the 1980s, the general reaction of most people to the hike in land prices was to fill every square centimetre and have as many rooms as possible. Land prices are still high, even in our long, continuing recession, but some people – my clients, at least – realize the importance of living with a garden space for their own well-being."

The architect continues, "Even if you fill the available space with floor, you can only be in one place at a time, and the sense of your surroundings is more important than being able to sit in every part of it. I don't see garden space as a luxury but as an essential antidote to the pressures of city life." Here, in Minato, one of Tokyo's expensive residential districts, Takayuki Houshuyama, an advertising creative director, and his wife Naoko, who works for a Japanese airline, calculated that they could just afford this

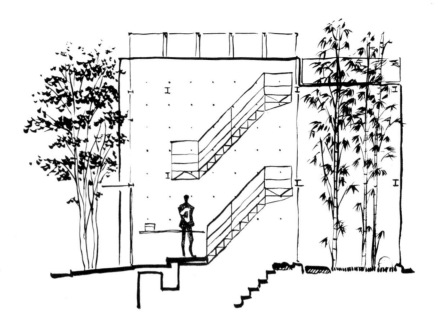

☾☽
A sketched side elevation shows the position of the light well on the right, at the south end of the house, and the relationship between the bamboo that fills the area and the Japanese stewartia near the front door.

☽
For an hour or two around midday, tall bamboos cast shadows across this textured-concrete wall. Near the bottom of the wall, two small openings, partly filled with cubic lights, open onto a narrow bed of dwarf azaleas. To the left is one of the sliding screens that give access to a *tatami* room on the ground floor.

41-square-metre (441 square feet) corner plot and have a house built on it by Sugiura. Perhaps surprisingly, the combined cost would have been the same as that of an apartment of an equivalent area – a much less attractive option. This saving is mainly achieved by the architect's ability to contain costs, and his use of economic construction materials, such as expanded-steel lathing.

At first sight of the plot, Naoko Houshuyama was doubtful. "It was no more than the parking space for two or three cars – and we needed to include a parking space for our own car." But, three days after they first met him, Sugiura had produced a design that delighted the couple. Central to it was a three-storey well with tall bamboo, visible from every part of the house. Small courtyard gardens (see pages 26–9) have a long history in Japanese and Chinese houses, and are more pertinent than ever in a closely packed urban environment that offers few exterior views. Nevertheless, the traditional *tsubo* occupies an area of some 3m x 3m (10ft x 10ft) – far too much of the space available here.

Sugiura devoted just 2.7m x 1.2m (8.9ft x 3.9ft) to the garden, but then extended this space the whole height of the house, naming it, with some irony, his *shaku-niwa – niwa* means garden, *shaku* an old Japanese unit of length equalling 37.8cm (14.9in). With a height of 5.5m (18ft), this pocket garden has a reasonable volume, but making it work depended on two things: filling it, and opening it to all angles of view and all three floors. Choosing the planting was easy, partly because the owners had a fondness for bamboo. *Phyllostachys pubescens*, one of the tallest bamboos, was imported into Japan from China in 1736 for the park of a prominent family but is now widespread. This species has a tiny "footprint" but a profusion of leaves all the way up its stem. To confine its growth, a concrete container was formed below ground level.

More critical was the distribution of light throughout the tall, narrow house, a consideration that went hand in hand with gaining maximum visibility of the bamboo. The long outer wall on the east side of the property gives directly onto a narrow street that doesn't even have a pavement, so a window here was ruled out for reasons of privacy. Instead, Sugiura drew light in from above, through the open garden well and a pitched skylight over the stairwell. White interior surfaces, including that of the inner garden wall, reflect the daylight, while glass screens and an open metal staircase give views of the bamboo. Outside, by the door, a Japanese stewartia (*Stewartia pseudocamellia*), chosen for its smooth, reddish trunk, and a dwarf azalea soften the exterior lines.

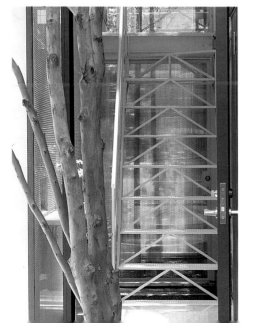

The middle portion of the tall stand of bamboo provides a soothing view of greenery for the living room on the first floor. When the sliding glass windows are pulled back, a mesh screen keeps insects out but allows air to circulate in the room.

With the front door open, it is possible to see straight through the entire length of the house, courtesy of the open design of the metal staircase. This view gives generous exposure to the bamboo, while a visual counterpoint is provided by the red trunk of the Japanese stewartia in the foreground.

house around a tree
design: denso sugiura

In this miniature house by Denso Sugiura in the fashionable district of Aoyama, a few minutes' walk from the boutiques and boulevard cafés of Omotesando, the dwelling is even more focused on a single natural feature than in the apartment and garden he designed in Minato (see pages 60–3). In this case the focus is a dogwood tree (*Cornus kousa*), a flowering species from the Japanese mountains. The owner of the house, Kazuyoshi Asakawa, won the tiny plot in an auction; it occupies the south-west corner of a residential block accessed by the narrow alleys typical of this part of central Tokyo, which are just wide enough for a single car to pass. The density of housing here is such that neighbours are only a few metres away, and there are no public spaces for trees.

Asakawa was, nevertheless, very keen to have a garden, or at least some sense of nature within the house. This was an important reason for choosing Sugiura to design the space. "I made a list for him with many, many requests. There were two things that were especially important to me. One was that we wanted to entertain on the ground floor – ideally to be able to have garden parties. The second was that the family living space should be concentrated on the first floor, yet still have nature appear there too."

The dimensions of the property are 6.7m by 4.2m (22ft by 13¾ft), giving an area of just over 28 square metres (300 square feet). Sugiura's idea was to have a tree rising the full height of the house, breaking through the first floor, and Asakawa chose a wild species of dogwood (*C. kousa*) that has a lot of seasonal variety. This tree was planted close to the front of the house for maximum visibility from the living areas, in a small, square plot surrounded by white-granite tiles. The ground floor is divided into two sections: the front garden of tiles and tree, and a raised platform that can be closed off with sliding screens,

>

The slim trunks of a dogwood (*Cornus kousa*) are the focus of the spare, white, interior garden. The small stone statues are modern versions of *O-jizo san*, traditional protector of children, and were carved by a sculptor friend of the family who live here.

◖

A square opening in the balcony offers a view down to the ground-floor garden. The restricted size of the opening helps to prevent the dogwood from spreading outwards. A few smaller trunks have been allowed to flourish, but these are pruned at intervals.

The berries of the dogwood, here just beginning to grow, lend the slender tree further visual appeal when they mature in the autumn. They also have a practical use as the source of a small quantity of liqueur.

During Tokyo's hot summers the balcony is kept cool by both the expanded-steel lathing that surrounds it and the spreading branches of the tree. The square wooden frame that protects the tree also does service as a bench.

A sketched rear elevation of the house (left) shows the view from the ground-floor room. When a party is held, the garden can be used as an extension of this space. The side elevation (right) shows the dogwood growing up through the front section of the house.

or left completely open to allow maximum use of the space. Sugiura recommended not fixing the use of this ground floor, but leaving it open and flexible. "In this way it can fulfil many uses. With such a small land area, this is the only sensible approach." When entertaining a few friends, the family use the platform for dining, and they have a view of the largely empty garden space; however, by taking over the entire ground floor, they can easily accommodate a party of a dozen.

Crucial to the success of this garden designed around a tree is Sugiura's special solution for the exterior walls, perfected in other houses in his *Chitchana* series (see page 60). He uses white, expanded-steel lathing, in two mesh densities, to give transparency and light. Although these panels are not the true walls of the house, they help to blur the distinction between inside and outside, and give a freer and more open feeling, while at the same time maintaining some privacy. Painted white, they light up when the sun strikes them, and they provide a clean backdrop to the branches and foliage of the dogwood. The tree grows up through a square opening cut in the wooden decking of the first-floor balcony to form part of a second garden, which is also enclosed by panels of steel lathing.

All of the lighting was carefully planned, and the lathing panels are a key component. Their degree of transparency depends on the time of day, the angle of the sun, and the balance between daylight and the interior artificial lighting. The spacing of the wooden planks on the floor of the balcony is wide enough to allow a play of chiaroscuro on the garden below in the middle of the day, while at night spotlights set in the square opening of the decking play on the base of the dogwood, and others reflect light from the lathing.

On the first floor, folding doors open the full width of the balcony and the deck abuts the main living room without a sill, so that the two areas merge. Surrounding the tree is a wooden bench, which becomes part of the general seating arrangement in fine weather. The square opening and bench also serve to confine the tree vertically; above here, it spreads and shows its seasonal changes. "I love this tree," Asakawa says. "In spring the buds are beautiful, followed by white flowers in May and June. During the summer there is plenty of shade from the leaves, and, when autumn comes, they turn reddish-brown, and there is a crop of berries." These last provide more than just a seasonal view of nature – Asakawa uses them to make his own berry liqueur.

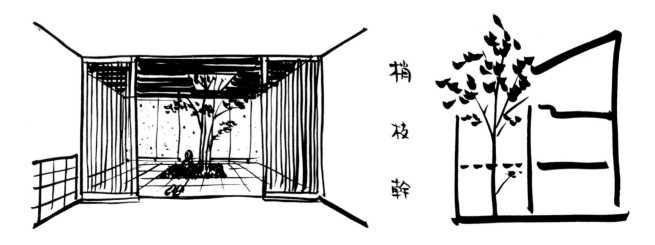

cherry-blossom focus
design: kosuke izumi

In a prime example of simplification, this garden in Hino, which lies about an hour and a half by train from Tokyo, is based around a single element: a cherry tree. To many gardeners in the West the traditional Japanese preference for simplicity and reduction sounds admirable in principle, but when faced with the practicalities of doing without these plants or those, few decide to carry it through. It even carries a hint of austerity and denial. In this case the choice of a single focus is even more extreme, since, for the Japanese, the key feature of the cherry is its blossom, and this is at its best for only a few days in the year. The custom of *hanami*, or "cherry-blossom viewing," is a national ritual, a celebration of the symbol of spring.

In fact, this concentration in Japan on one important emblem of nature serves to heighten its appreciation. The experience includes not only the pleasure of seeing the tree in full bloom, but the anticipation leading up to early April, and the reflection afterwards, when the blossoms gradually fall onto the black pebbles underneath. Of course, this does not mean that the garden is without value for the remainder of the year – that spring only brings a peak of enjoyment. A tall maple planted right outside the house spreads its branches over the wall, so that in autumn the changing of its leaves from green to red can also be enjoyed; these too eventually drop onto the pebbles.

The tree plays a central role in a garden that celebrates naturalness, in however sparse a manner. The architect, Kosuke Izumi, is well known in Japan for his part in the promotion of the return to the use of natural materials, which he champions in lectures and articles. It was after they attended one of his lectures that the owners decided to ask him to design their new home. The name of the house, Doro-outzu, refers to a traditional mud-plastering technique that involves the addition of lime. The lime both strengthens the render and lightens it in tone, and Izumi was keen to revive the tradition in a modern home. Here, in texture and colour, the mud plaster sets the tone for a restrained but light-filled garden.

Certain key features of the house are designed to promote enjoyment of the garden, which is revealed by stages. The first view for a visitor stepping inside the front door is of this low opening, which displays nothing more than a bed of black pebbles.

The severely restricted perspective offered by this low opening makes it almost impossible to resist kneeling in order to see more. Doing so reveals most of the surface area of the garden, although still only a partial view of the cherry tree is granted.

Walking along the corridor, the visitor becomes aware of a row of circular holes at eye level. These penetrate the thick wall, and each one gives a tiny framed view of a few blossoms on the cherry tree. Along with the view through the low opening shown above, this glimpse helps the guest to build up a mental picture of the tree before it can be seen in its entirety.

A full view of the cherry blossom in all its April glory is available only from the living room, once the walk along the corridor has built up a sense of anticipation. The large trough in which the black pebbles lie can be filled in about twenty minutes to create a pond.

The tea-ceremony room lies across the garden from the living room and has its own geometric view of the garden, produced by the grid pattern of the sliding screens. After the square concrete stepping stones have been crossed, access to the tiny room is gained through the traditional "wriggling-in entrance" at bottom right.

The traditional drainage trough that runs under the eaves at the edge of the garden is extended close to the entrance, where the cherry tree stands, to make a pebble pond. The pond is designed to offer two varieties of space: one is a shallow pool, the other a bed of dry pebbles. This variability, easily controlled by means of a corner drain, is similar to that used in the garden in Osaka designed by Yasujirou Aoki, Chitoshi Kihara, and Masa Tada (see pages 132–5), and hints at the traditional precincts of Shinto shrines. Crossing from the grassy area to the pebble pond, a path of square-cut stones leads to a small tea-ceremony room situated next to the main entrance of the house.

Izumi regards gardens as an essential responsibility of the architect. "I love plants and trees, and incorporate them into all of my house designs," he says. From the time when he was a student visiting the gardens of Kyoto and Nara to research the plantings, he has paid close attention to the role played by individual trees. "After we have brought in a tree, I take time to reassess the garden. Trees have personality in the same way as do stones, and sometimes they suggest changes to the design." It took time to find the right specimen, a *shidare-zakura*, or weeping cherry, as Izumi needed a tree that would grow into a shape that accorded with the dimensions at this end of the garden. Once the weeping cherry had been planted, Izumi altered the layout of the pebble pond slightly. One of his intentions was that during the spring the blossoms would gradually fall onto the black pebbles and make an attractive colour combination. Now, after five years, he considers that the tree has reached its ideal shape, and from now on it will be pruned carefully.

The central importance of the cherry tree in traditional Japanese gardening demands control of the sequence in which it is experienced. Here, the visitor, entering through the main gate, faces a corridor of rendered mud and lime – used in the *doro-outzu* technique, which gave the house its name – that leads to the door of the house. On the left is the garden, but the view of this is tightly controlled to stimulate interest. It is blocked by a wall under which a 1m- (3ft-) high gap was left; this wall runs the length of the corridor and reveals, from a standing position, just the bed of pebbles. Set at head height in the wall is a series of small, circular openings that invite the visitor to peer through, and each of these gives a view of a small detail of branch and flowers. Only when the visitor goes inside the living room can the entire tree be seen. On the opposite side of the house, the tea-ceremony room offers yet another view.

austerity of line and colour
design: ikuma shirai

The function of this property in the mountains about an hour's drive from the city of Hiroshima is a little unusual. The owner is a famous *soba*-noodle chef from Yamanashi, north of Tokyo, who chose this area for a country retreat where he could not only relax and enjoy the scenery, but also make and serve noodles. *Soba* are the traditional Japanese buckwheat noodles cut by hand into square-sectioned strands, as distinct from *ramen*, which are of Chinese origin. While this is not the place to explain the mysteries and importance of noodles in Japanese culture, they are the passion of this client, and the reason for the name of this house and garden – Sekkasanbo ("snow flower") – alludes to the white flower of the *soba* plant. Moreover, in a way that perhaps only the Japanese would think of, the story of *soba* has a direct bearing on the simplicity – even austerity – of the garden. *Soba* is regarded as an extremely traditional Japanese food – pure and simple, and therefore difficult to make perfectly; it is also a food of the common people because buckwheat can grow on almost barren land, where rice or barley would be impossible to cultivate.

The architect, Ikuma Shirai, considered the location – a natural terrace on the mountainside – carefully. Clearly important would be the view, of both the distant mountain skyline and the nearer forest on the slope below. In fact, it seemed to Shirai that, with such dominant natural surroundings, it would be better not to attempt to compete with them in the design for the garden. "Against this nature, an artificial garden could not win." A first decision, therefore, was that the Sekkasanbo garden would complement the natural view by means of colour and line, and would extend to it visually.

To give the maximum view, Shirai had the plot levelled flat, which had the additional advantage of removing any distractions from the foreground. He then decided to dispense altogether with a wall on the southern and western sides, which face downhill, and to use

A row of tall bamboos screens the house and garden from the upper slope on the southern side of the property. The sophisticated curves of the roof, that dominate the design of the house, echo the profiles of the surrounding mountains and are also mirrored in the concave western border of the garden.

Seen here from the steps that lead to the front entrance, pink azaleas planted along the south edge of the garden create a lower frame for a view of a conifer forest beyond. The colour of the flowers also combines elegantly with the grey stone and gravel.

The design of the garden has been honed to great
simplicity, and focuses on parallel bands of colour
and texture – the concrete sill, the rainwater trough
filled with black pebbles, raked gravel, and azaleas.
Contrast of line is provided by the tension between
the straight lines formed by these elements and the
broad curves of the roof and porch.

On the north side of the house, within the veranda, is
a water fountain of black granite with a surrounding
pebble trough. The granite's surface reflects two
components of the garden beyond – the stand of
bamboo and a single cherry tree.

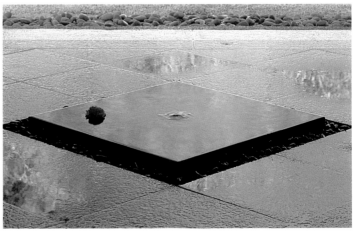

two low borders instead. On the south side he set out a straight line of low azalea shrubs to make a lower frame for the forest trees; on the west he laid a gentle curve of flat stones.

Another strong influence on the garden was the roofline of the main building, into which Shirai invested special effort. It combines, in an original and subtle manner, three curves, originating from two traditional styles of roof. In section, the principal curve is convex and shallow, as is the curve of the edges in a plan view in a seventeenth-century style known as *Mukuri*. Superimposed on these is a slight convexity at the corners – an upward warp typical of the *Nokizori* style used for temples. The two elements were never combined, but Shirai inherited a deep knowledge of traditional building techniques from his father, Seiichi Shirai, one of the most influential architects of the early twentieth century.

The garden therefore occupies an intermediate position, visually and conceptually, between the soft lines of the surrounding mountain landscape and the subtle but strong character of the building's roof in the centre. Almost the entire surface is covered with *shirakawasuna* – what the Japanese call "white river sand", but is actually a fine, evenly textured gravel. Raked in parallel lines, it expresses water in the tradition of the *karesansui*, or dry-stone garden (see pages 18–21), but in an even more austere way than that of a Zen garden, which would typically have stone arrangements set within it.

A single path of stepping stones breaks through this broad surround on the west side and leads up to the main entrance, while on the north, facing uphill and bordered by a fence and a line of tall bamboos, Shirai planted a single *shidare-zakura*, or weeping cherry, to provide an accent for the view from the bedroom. A trough lined with black pebbles drains rainwater from the roof, and forms the inner border to the gravel garden. The rigorous simplicity of the plain raked gravel, and its size relative to the building at its centre, recall the formality and ritual of Shinto shrines, with their pebble-strewn precincts. Its barren whiteness suggests the *soba* plant – hence the name given by Shirai.

The main entrance to the house is on the west side, where the garden is bounded only by a long, curved border of stones, visible here in the foreground. Leading to the door are stepping stones – the only feature to break up the expanse of raked gravel.

The original plan shows that the designer had intended to have trees in the north-west and south-west corners of the garden. However, he finally favoured greater austerity, and now the only tree is a single cherry in the centre of the north side, close to the wall.

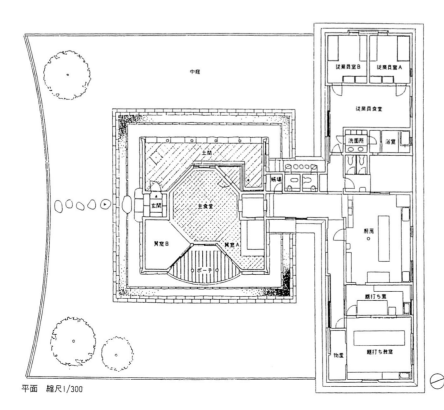

平面　縮尺1/300

The design of the courtyard on the fourth floor focuses on a group of five stones that symbolize the five peaks of the cosmic mountain of Buddhist mythology. Carved into the face of the second stone from the right is a circle that represents the sun; a crescent on the stone behind it stands for the moon.

The various elements of the garden are integrated into the design in such a way that, from particular viewpoints, they form harmonious compositions. One such composition, seen here from the path, occurs on the balcony terrace close to the courtyard. A horizontally trained branch of a maple follows the line of an elliptically shaped mound of moss, while stones curve around the mound to the right.

an oasis for contemplation
design: shunmyo masuno

The business district of Kojimachi in central Tokyo contains offices and some of the better-known large hotels – not an unpleasant place by city standards, but nevertheless not one that lends itself to the evocation of nature. As Shunmyo Masuno, a Zen priest and acknowledged master of the modern Zen garden, says, "Groupings of trees, decorative water features and colourful garden beds adorning buildings and parks cannot be recognized as nature." It is, he considers, a "harsh environment" that "creates a state of constant hurriedness for its inhabitants."

A new hotel constructed for an association of prefectural government employees offered the opportunity to take remedial action. Masuno believes in extending the role of the Zen garden beyond temple grounds, and to achieve this he has undertaken a number of large projects, including museums, libraries, hotels, and a national technology institute. Here, at the Kojimachi Kaikan hotel, he had available three spaces: two on the fourth floor, much used for wedding receptions, and a ground-floor site next to the coffee shop and reception area.

A Zen garden is functional, and the purpose of this grouping of three terraces, Masuno explains, is to give visitors who are there for a typically short visit "a substantial experience of the moment." Our motion in life is stopped occasionally when we come across unique moments of nature. For example, it could be one that "expresses a prolonged tolerance of the hardships of nature," as he puts it, "or a glorious landscape that reflects and reveals the power and beauty of nature." Such opportunities to experience this kind of emotional response rarely occur in urban environments, where ironically the need for them is great, as is the contrast they make with the pressure and speed of city life.

The challenge was to create a natural atmosphere for contemplation and for revitalization of the spirit. Having studied the site very carefully so that he could sense fully its needs and possibilities, Masuno started with the basic concept of "a vision of absolute peacefulness, as if one were deep within the forested mountains." The three spaces would combine to create one garden, and would be called Seizan-Ryokusui no Niwa – The Garden of Blue Mountains and Green Water. This name, however, also carries a hidden meaning that gives a clue to the underlying Buddhist symbolism that informs the project. As well as referring to "Blue Mountains," *Seizan* means Nirvana, while *Ryokusui* ("Green Water") is an expression for nature.

The placement of rocks also makes reference to Buddhist cosmology and symbolism, in which odd numbers play a significant part. There are, for instance, the Three Worlds; also the five peaks of the cosmic mountain at the centre of the universe, Mount Sumeru (*Shumi-sen* in Japanese), and the seven golden mountain ranges and seas that surround it concentrically. "Odd numbers are felicitous – *kichijyosu* – and in the fourth-floor courtyard I placed eleven rocks in three groups of five, three and three." A stream is represented by small stones issuing from the base of one rock, on which is chiselled a crescent, representing the moon. On the other side of the central mossy mound, one of the group of five rocks is carved with a circle, representing the sun. Thus, as in Buddhist cosmology, the sun and moon revolve around the cosmic mountain. The two principal trees of the garden are the mountain maple (*Acer matsumurae*), and the Japanese ash

These are new spring shoots on a young Japanese maple (*Acer palmatum*) on the fourth-floor balcony terrace. For Japanese gardeners, one of the attractions of this tree is the variety of colour changes in the leaves, which differ according to the species and also on the soil composition (neutral and acid soils tend to give deeper reds).

(*Fraxinus japonica*). The latter, which comes from the north of Japan's main island, Honshu, and will grow to a height of more than 6m (20ft), is traditionally used for divining water, and is a symbol of good fortune.

In both Japanese and Chinese art, mountains are inseparable from water – hence the dry representation by means of carefully graded stones and gravel. The main floor area at the Kojimachi Kaikan, however, offered a space where real water could be used, and here Masuno took full advantage of this to create both a pool and waterfalls, filling the view from the window of the coffee shop, for which it is, he explains, "a proxy *tokonama*." In a Japanese tea-ceremony room, the *tokonoma* is an alcove in which are placed objects of aesthetic significance, such as a scroll painting, a flower in a special holder, or a *suiseki* – a small, naturally formed stone admired for its beauty and its power to suggest a scene from nature or an object closely associated with nature. Here, Masuno laid a shallow pond directly in front of the window to represent the floor of the *tokonoma*, arranging within it a series of dynamically cut stones; there are eleven of these, just as in the courtyard garden. The backdrop, the equivalent of a scroll painting, is a waterfall terrace of two kinds of stone. The lower section, of brown-granite rocks, supports layers of thinly sliced slabs of black South African granite, which are carefully chiselled at the edges to turn the flow of water into a sparkling cascade.

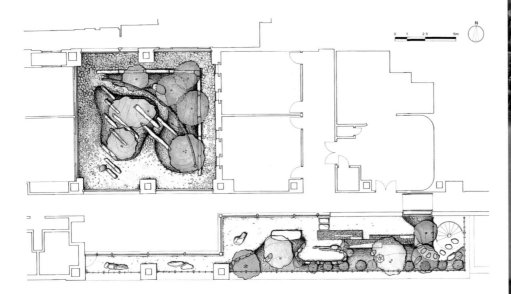

This plan shows the two gardens on the fourth floor. Their separation was dictated by the space available.

❮
On the lobby level is the water garden, where the form of hewn granite stones echoes the diagonal lines of the imposing wall that encloses the space.

❮❮
Brown-granite stones support thin slices of black granite to create a wall down which a waterfall cascades into the water garden's shallow pool.

the symbolism of rocks
design: shunmyo masuno

The Canadian Embassy in Tokyo occupies a commanding yet attractive site in Aoyama, opposite the grounds of Akasaka Palace and next to a wooded park, Takahashi Memorial Gardens. Completed in 1991, it features a broad, upper-level terrace that looks out over these green spaces, and it was decided to give this over to a garden that would be in some way appropriate to the function of the embassy. The project was entrusted to Shunmyo Masuno, who immediately saw that the garden had to relate to the people who worked in and with the embassy, and to those who came to visit. Through his priest's training and long experience of Zen gardens, Masuno understands the importance of purpose in garden design. Just as a Zen temple garden is a means of spiritual expression for the priest who makes it, and an aid to meditation for those who visit and experience it, so Masuno's modern gardens have a specific function.

The function in this case was, according to Masuno, "to encourage the people whose job it is to link and liaise between the two nations to reappraise their roles." From this concept, it was a natural step to plan a garden that would symbolize the relationship between the two countries. In fact, he decided on two linked gardens: the larger space representing Canada; and the smaller one symbolizing Japan. The representational techniques already developed for *karesansui*, dry-stone gardens (see pages 18–21) were ideal for such a thematic approach, and Masuno adapted them so as to be able to show the key natural features of a large continent and its surrounding oceans.

Masuno's love of stone led him to emphasize the geology of Canada in his design. Leading from a pond that represents the Atlantic Ocean in the south-east corner, the ancient rocks of the Canadian Shield are symbolized by granite stones brought from Hiroshima prefecture. During his research on the Canadian landscape, Masuno was impressed by the effect of the Ice Age, and, to convey the idea of a land gouged by glaciers, he left the stones as they had split.

The longest span of the rock garden is the Canada Garden, on the eastern terrace, overhung by the projecting roof of the country's embassy in Tokyo. The large stones, roughly hewn and with rows of wedge holes left untouched, symbolize the geologically ancient Canadian Shield. The Rocky Mountains are represented by the pyramids in the distance.

Around the corner and to the left of the view opposite is a still pond that represents the Pacific Ocean. In a deliberate illusion of perspective, the stone jetty in the foreground tapers to a point in the middle of the pond. To complete the view, the trees in the grounds of Akasaka Palace are "borrowed," in accordance with the ancient tradition of *shakkei* (see pages *34–9*).

Masuno's stonemason for this project, as for many others, was Masatoshi Izumi, who enthuses about this raw, exposed treatment. "Large and small waves of pattern and colour decorate the surface of the stone, while the split edges look like sheer cliffs and contrast so beautifully with the natural unsplit surfaces of the stone. Then there are the grooves left by the wedges that split it, and if it is polished, the stone takes on a new disposition and lustre. In fact, given the necessary skills and a full understanding of the potentials, it is possible to produce a stone with a beauty and charm completely different from those of the naturally occurring type." To overcome the structural problem of these stones' great weight, they were laboriously hollowed out.

The horizontality of the laid stones, combined with the considerable depth of the terrace, effectively evokes the immense scale of the Canadian landscape, and the massive overhang of the roof compresses the visual frame into a panorama. Beyond, the treetops of Akasaka Palace to the north and north-east, and those of the Takahashi Memorial Gardens to the east merge imperceptibly, and are in effect "borrowed" to add a band of green nature to the scene.

At the far corner, the garden turns at an *inukshuk*, or marker symbol, of the Inuit people of Canada's Arctic. Next to this, three pyramidal blocks of different sizes traverse part of the north edge, representing the Rocky Mountains. Finally, in the north-west corner, is another expanse of water, symbolizing the Pacific Ocean, and, from here, a small corridor leads into the second garden – that representing Japan. With its natural stones surrounded by raked gravel and traversed by stepping stones, this is actually a form of Zen garden. The stepping stones are highly ordered in geometric patterns, even though they incorporate natural stones, and this linear control helps to create a deliberately "tense atmosphere amid the delicacy and detailing." At the far end of this garden, a massive stone in two halves is a summation of the relationship between Canada and Japan – as Masuno puts it, "by being balanced and by being kept slightly apart."

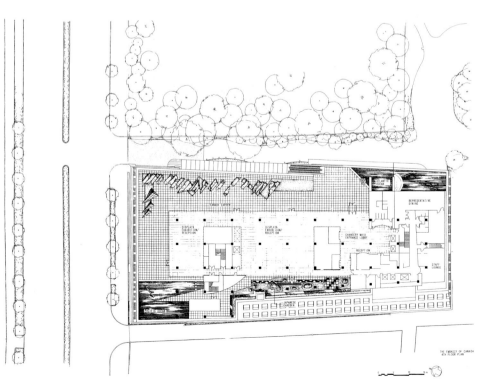

The plan of this intermediate floor of the Canadian Embassy, most of which is taken up by the two gardens that surround a glass-walled central lobby and exhibition area. The sequence of the gardens begins in the south-east corner, at top right, with a pond that represents the Atlantic Ocean. The visitor progresses northwards, passing through an extensive garden representing Canada, as far as the Pacific Pond in the bottom left corner, and finally heads southwards through the more formal Japan Garden.

At the far end of the Japan Garden, a precise
chequerboard of stepping stones indicates formality
and control – aspects of the Japanese character.
The two halves of the split stone standing in front
of the wall represent the relationship between the
two nations of Canada and Japan.

Stone islands set in raked gravel evoke a Zen garden
such as that of the famous Ryoan-ji temple in Kyoto.
Not only is this arrangement powerfully symbolic of
Japan, but, in the view of the designer, Zen itself
underpins the country's culture and way of thinking.

The view of this "garden as painting" has been enhanced by the use of a single sheet of glass instead of a sliding window, with its inevitable stanchions that detract from the scene. In addition, the light levels in this living room are carefully controlled and the lighting fittings positioned in such a way that the glass is largely without reflection and the view of the garden is sparklingly clear.

modern machiya
design: yoshihiro mashiko

Traditional Japanese town houses, which can still be found in parts of Kyoto, had a narrow frontage to the street, but considerable depth. These *machiya*, as they are known, present some obvious difficulties for constructing a garden, which can only be long and thin, so that they are viewed from close up. One solution was to have more than one garden – small, naturally – in different parts of the house.

For different reasons, a similar problem was faced by a family planning a house on a plot close to Ueno Park, in Tokyo. The owner, Yuji Tezuka, is a successful painter of modern Japanese landscapes, executed on a large scale; he needed a large studio, which the architect, Yoshihiro Mashiko, planned for the first floor, and which takes up most of the width of the plot. The living area is underneath, on the ground floor, and the only space available for a garden was a narrow rectangle. A further problem was the reduction of light caused by the location of the house right next to another three-storey dwelling.

Considering the restricted dimensions, both architect and owner agreed that the garden should be a place to be viewed rather than one in which to walk or sit. Accordingly, Mashiko designed the living-cum-dining room so that it would have maximum frontage onto the garden, and this side was fitted with a wide picture window. The essential difficulty, however, was what kind of garden to present to the interior, given that it would be a constant scene. The parallels between this lateral garden and the owner's landscape paintings were obvious, and Mashiko was sensitive to the need for a view that would be neither too insistent in its components, nor become boring. A second consideration was any method of redirecting light into the living area, and a third was that the majority of the plants would have to be shade-loving, because of the limited sunlight reaching the garden.

At first Tezuka tried painting a backdrop himself directly onto a plaster wall, but as he and his wife became used to living in the new house, they found it too over-powering, and Tezuka decided that a pure garden, professionally executed, would make a break from his own work. On Mashiko's advice, he contracted Iwaki Zoen, one of the oldest and largest gardening contractors in Japan, who normally do much larger projects. The painted wall was replaced with a bamboo screen, and most of this was left uncovered by plants, both to reflect light into the room and to create a minimal effect. As Tezuka explains, "It's important for me that there should be no strong focus of attention in the garden. If it had strong colours, my eyes would take them to the studio when I start to paint. I needed a garden without impact that I could look at every day and for ever."

The screen, with its black cord ties, represents an outline landscape from the perspective of Japanese painting, in which horizontal layers are piled up and repeated, as in rice terracing on a mountainside. The ties are tied in the random pattern known as *ranmusubi*. In the bed below the screen, and faced with stone, are various shade-loving plants. These include sacred or heavenly bamboo (*Nandina domestica*), Japanese spurge (*Pachysandra terminalis*), pieris (*Pieris japonica*), and *kitchijouso* (*Reineckea carnea*), a perennial native herb with a pale-purple flower. The trees, framing the scene left and right, are maple, blue Japanese oak (*Quercus glauca*), flowering dogwood (*Cornus kousa*), and spike winter hazel (*Corylopsis spicata*), a low, deciduous tree with pale-yellow flowers in spring.

One of the roles of this small garden is to serve as inspiration for the owner's paintings. Thus, a maple, which embodies so much of the Japanese concept of landscape, was an essential ingredient in the view.

A small, triangular space at the front of the house has been turned into a modern version of a *genkan-niwa* – the tiny garden near the entrance that is a part of the *machiya* tradition of dividing the garden.

reflections in steel, glass, and water

design: yasujirou aoki and chitoshi kihara

This garden, completed in 2001, surrounds a bright, contemporary treatment of a tea-ceremony room, executed in glass and steel. Since it embodies so much that is unique in Japanese culture, the tea-ceremony room represents an interesting creative challenge for modern architects and designers. Osaka-based architect Chitoshi Kihara was able here to display his reinterpretation, and asked his long-term collaborator Yasujirou Aoki to design an appropriate garden.

The design of the tea-ceremony room largely controlled the garden space. Kihara wanted the walls to be of etched glass, unbroken by a load-bearing frame, and the solution was to support the roof projection separately with pillars. To keep the glass walls visually light, Kihara moved the two pillars further out, which produced a greater roof overhang, and reduced their thickness by using two L-sectioned girders corner to corner for each. In an imaginative stroke, he clad the pillars with mirror-surfaced stainless steel, so that from certain angles they create the illusion of disappearing into the surrounding garden.

To soften and lighten the extent of the overhang, Kihara made it circular, and this set the scene for an interplay of curves and straight lines in the garden below. The pebbled rainwater trough underneath is curved, and he added a curved outer wall, which intersects with one corner of the tea-ceremony room. In this space, which is roughly a quadrant of a circle, Aoki decided to put a shallow pond, over which the tea-ceremony room would be cantilevered slightly. The pond and its attached arrangement of plants and rocks would symbolize a landscape, but Aoki, like Shunmyo Masuno and generations

The view towards the narrow end of the Frog Pond looks out over the pebble beach and embraces the vertical slits in the curved outer wall. Jutting out of the water is the stone that inspired the pond's name.

Stainless-steel cladding lightens the appearance of one of the pillars supporting the overhanging roof. The multiple reflections created by the polished surface add an illusory touch to the garden.

Shoji screens and their openings are used to provide
a controlled view from inside the tea-ceremony room.
The view to the left takes in the vertical slits in the
wall and, beyond them, the outer garden. Also
included in the careful composition of this interior
space are the "frog" stone, one of the reflecting
pillars, and a corner of the pebble beach.

of Japanese gardeners before him, designs his gardens one step at a time. Instead of working it all out in detail first, then laying it down at once, he selects his stones and plants one by one, "listening" to what they prefer. Engaging in a dialogue with the components of a garden is an acknowledged Japanese approach, dating back at least to the original classic manual of garden-making, the late-eleventh-century *Shakutai-ki*, which advises the reader to "follow the request" of the stone. Aoki first selected a single stone for the pond, choosing its position in relation to the view through the screens of the tea-ceremony room. He realized that it resembled a frog, and this suggested the name the Frog Pond.

Small pebbles were needed for the pond bed, and Aoki set these in concrete, some of them spiralling around the stone. The convergence of the curved wall and the straight edge of the tea-ceremony room at the back of the property created a wedge shape, and here Aoki decided on a beach backed by miniature mountains. To achieve this, he made the pond bed slope upwards, adding larger pebbles for the beach. Completing the landscape are brown-granite stones, with a planting of ferns, a maple, a camellia (*Camellia lutchuensis*), and a blue Japanese oak (*Quercus glauca*). This selection acknowledges the *inyo* principle of negative and positive energy – the camellia and oak look backwards towards the negative space at the end, while the maple looks out across to the pond and its broader opening – the direction of the positive flow of energy. At this opening, facing the house, stand a *natsuhaze* tree (*Vaccinium oldhamii*) and a Japanese yew (*Taxus cuspidata*); beyond these is a plain grass lawn.

As would be expected, the views from the tea-ceremony room, adjustable by means of a sliding door (the "wriggling-in entrance") and *shoji* screens, are worked out carefully. The view through the small door takes in a series of narrow vertical gaps in the outer curved wall, which give onto the small outer garden. The view through the *shoji* screens that open onto the pond takes in the curved wall, one of the bright, reflecting pillars, and, depending on the sitter's position, either the "frog" stone or the pebble beach. With no planting actually in the pond, Aoki felt that something else was needed, and decided, in a radical move for the tea ceremony, to hang the traditional flower arrangement in its basket on the outer wall, rather than in or next to the *tokonoma* inside.

A yew tree, at bottom left, looks across the Frog Pond to a miniature landscape of maple, camellia, and blue oak at the far end of the pool, glimpsed through the tea-ceremony room. This curving arrangement is designed to direct the flow of positive energy out from the pond towards the yew.

❧

At this side entrance to the museum, tiles are used as architectural decoration, as paving, and to provide a contrast with the texture and colour of the plants. Roof-ridge tiles framing the gateway are arranged to mirror the culms of the black bamboo planted along one of the walls near the entrance, while tumbled tile fragments give a softer appearance to the path.

☾

A turtle constructed from old, cracked tiles is one of several interpretations of creatures embedded in the pathways on the far side of the museum's garden. In this space the designer expressed playful ideas that contrast with the formality of the main entrance.

tiles express an old aesthetic
design: kan izue

The town of Omihachiman in Shiga prefecture, close to the eastern shore of Lake Biwa, became famous in the seventeenth century for the manufacture of *kawara*, traditional Japanese clay tiles. An old factory in the historic part of the town was scheduled for demolition, but a public outcry at a proposal to replace it with high-rise apartments led the council to plan a *kawara* museum instead. The winner of the design competition was Kan Izue, who had some original ideas about how the museum should appear, including the function of the associated garden.

Izue, born in 1931, has often seemed to be iconoclastic, and is certainly no stranger to controversy. Perhaps his best-known creation is the 1994 Bou-Bou-an tea house in Nagoya, with walls of zinc, embossed iron plate of the kind used for manhole covers at the entrance, and walls plastered with old newspapers and a photograph of a naked woman – not at all what one would expect for the refined Japanese tea ceremony. Yet it was a brave attempt to return to the *sukiya* ideal of the tea ceremony's creator, Sen-no-Rikyu, who wanted to make the ritual available to the common people who had access only to cheap materials, and the design was awarded an International Academy of Architecture Prize. The philosophy behind this building, *shin-gyou-sou*, goes a long way to explain Izue's other work, such as here at the tile museum in Omihachiman.

The *shin-gyou-sou* aesthetic was created in the fifteenth century by a Zen priest called Ikkyu, and is applied to the arts of calligraphy, flower arrangement, poetry, and garden design. Meaning approximately "strictly formal-softer-free," it represents a transition between these three states, and was based on Ikkyu's own life experience. As a young man in Kyoto he was compelled to enter the priesthood to avoid death at the orders of the shogun, so for many years he followed the strict, harsh lifestyle of Zen training – *shin*.

The front door of the museum is approached by a long, broad path that Izue has set with interlocking patterns made of tiles, most of which are inserted so that only the outer edges appear on the surface. With the exception of a spiral motif (above left), just in front of the entrance, like an ammonite uncovered in geological strata, the patterns here are regimented and emphasize both straight lines set at right angles to each other and diagonal lines (above).

The garden begins with a formal and hard style. This quality, described as *shin* in Japanese, is exemplified by the precise geometry of paving tiles laid out in diamond and triangular patterns, and by a row of black bamboo (*Phyllostachys nigra*), that lines one wall and is backed by regularly spaced, vertical motifs.

The second phase of his life was softer and more secular – *gyou* – and as an older man he enjoyed a life of freedom – *sou*. The famous seventeenth-century Japanese gardener Enshu Kobori employed *shin-gyou-sou* in his use of stone in the garden of Kyoto's Daitoku temple, where Ikkyu was the resident priest. Here, in the garden of this tile museum, Izue uses the same transitional aesthetic, but employs broken tiles instead of stone. He wants visitors to experience the three states of *shin-gyou-sou* as they walk through the sections of garden that link the buildings, appreciating both the contrast and the connections between the three.

The approach to the museum is straight and narrow, to conform with the hard, stoic state of *shin*. To reinforce this, the only planting is a row of non-flowering black bamboo *Phyllostachys nigra*), along one white wall, and a row of even more severe vertical strips of black tiles. The black-bamboo theme is also picked up by vertical tiers of curved tiles at the doorways to resemble bamboo stems. The contrasting final state of freedom – *sou* – is represented by such trees as willows, maples, and weeping cherry, together with grass, and the softening transition between the two – *gyou* – is carried by the tile mosaics that Izue has made his speciality.

Naturally, tiles are central to the purpose of the museum, but the ones that Izue chose and collected for the garden paving are not the efficient modern variety but old, broken *kawara* tiles from the 1995 Hanshin earthquake that devastated Kobe. To Izue, these tiles, with their high rate of water absorption, harmonize with nature, acquiring moss and a patchy coloration – in short, they mature gracefully and softly. Since they soak up a substantial amount of water, *kawara* tiles are likely to crack or break apart when they freeze in winter. Tiles are still widely used in Japan for roofs, but the modern variety are impermeable. Nevertheless, for Izue, only the old kind have character. In creating the paving, he has made a marvellous variety of patterns – geometric and formal close to the entrance, changing to free-form, flowing arrangements, and playful representations of fish, turtles, flowers, and birds. Between the building and the willow and cherry trees, a large carp executed in tiles helps to make the *gyou* transition.

The *shin-gyou-sou* aesthetic that directs the gardens and pathways may be a little obscure, but it gives a coherence to the experience of visiting the museum, and a sense of development. Izue likes to use another analogy for *shin-gyou-sou*, that of calligraphy. The stoic, correct *shin* is represented by the clearly executed style that contains all of the strokes of a character; *gyou* is represented by the looser, but easily readable, style that most people use when writing by hand; and the free *sou* is represented by the more individualistic freestyle, as used for signatures. This may seem more than a little removed from garden design, but in a curious way Izue has used tiles and plants in this garden to create a kind of calligraphic imagery, with branches, leaves, and the edges of the *kawara* tiles as the brushstrokes.

At the far end of the garden, next to the canal, the softness of the *sou* style is embodied in both the horizontal and the vertical plane. Representation of birds and fishes, including a giant carp in the left foreground, are set on the ground within a free-form pattern of tiles. Above this stands a group of weeping cherry, willow, and maple trees.

the garden as female principle
design: kan izue

Not far from Omihachiman's tile museum (see pages 94–7), Kan Izue has also recently completed a residence for a local businessman. For once in this densely populated country, shortage of land was not a problem, and so the architect was free to experiment with the garden. Here, not only do the plants play a sculptural and even an architectural role, but they also have symbolic significance.

In plan, the house and garden are interlaced to give a first impression of something like a small hamlet; this is heightened by the location which borders rice fields, with a stream running along one wall. Crossing a small bridge to enter the property, the visitor finds a winding corridor flanking a stand of bamboo on one side, a camellia tree on another side, and the ground all paved with Izue's signature patterns of old *kawara* tiles. His passion for diverse materials is evident in his imaginative juxtapositions of oxidized iron, etched glass, concrete, polished black wood, and screens of hanging chains. To this variety of artificial materials, the plants add their own texture, form, and colour.

This is not simply a random contrast intended to achieve an obvious visual effect. Izue's idea goes deeper, to present a unity of contrasts – in fact, yin and yang, man and woman. As he says, "The garden expresses woman, the house expresses man. It is a set." The yin–yang principle applied to gardens is by no means new, and can be seen in the combinations of male and female rocks so popular in the "stroll gardens" of the Edo period (1603–1868). Izue, however, has made the entire garden represent the female, its softer components contrasting with the harder materials and lines of the buildings (although glass, for idiosyncratic reasons, is feminine to Izue, and so the extensive windows are a kind of interface in this man-and-woman combination).

Each material – including the plants – plays a part in this concept. For example, on the east side of the house, facing the street, the angle between two walls forms a long, triangular slope, and here Izue has planted a Japanese maple (*Acer palmatum*), soft and yellow-leafed, against the severe, vertical, concrete projections. Underneath, he planted bamboo grass (*Shibataea kumasasa*), again for the softness of its small, broad leaves and

The contrast between hard (masculine) and soft (feminine) begins at the exterior of the garden. Maples and bamboo grass are treated like architectural materials, chosen for delicate textures that contrast with the rigid verticals and horizontals of the walls and their concrete projections.

Kan Izue is dedicated to recycling old Japanese roof tiles for artistic use. He creates paving patterns by inserting the tiles into the earth, usually in such a way that just the edges show, and then filling the spaces between them with gravel.

The circular guest bedroom has its own surrounding garden, as can also be seen on the plan on page 101. The bedroom is a main visual focus for the rest of the house, and is highly visible from the glass-walled corridor. A star-shaped pattern of grass and tile is arranged around the room's circumference, while the Narihira bamboo (*Semiarundinaria fastuosa*) has been pruned to roof height and trimmed into clusters.

its slender culms. Inside the house, he avoided more masculine trees, such as pines, choosing instead camellias, while around the exterior of the circular bedroom, he planted a stand of tall bamboo (*Semiarundinaria fastuosa*) and *ryunohige* grass.

The non-planted areas of the garden are paved in a manner similar to that at the tile museum, with fragments of old *kawara* tiles salvaged from the Kobe earthquake of 1995. Even these contribute to the feminine aspect of the garden. "One of the reasons I used them here was precisely because they were broken. I am recycling them, and recycling means rebirth." There are at least forty different shapes of traditional *kawara*, to fit the different parts of different styles of roof, from the simply curved tiles that overlap each other on the main sections, to the half-cylindrical cappings for the ridges, and the elaborate, gargoyle-like finials that decorate the gable ends. All of this provides a rich palette with which to compose patterns.

Izue has a special affection for these old tiles, and for him they are what he calls a "silent" material, like stone. Full of history, they also weather and become more attractive with the passage of time – Izue interprets the Japanese word *utsukushi*, which means "beautiful," as containing the quality of ageing gracefully. Tiles are still used, particularly in the countryside, but techniques have improved so that modern tiles do not absorb water and therefore do not crack in winter – in Izue's view, a purely functional improvement. One of his treatments for tile fragments, which he uses to accelerate their "ageing" and soften their form for paving, is to tumble them with sand in a cement mixer.

Old *kawara* tiles are embedded in the ground throughout the garden, in all the spaces between plantings. The sheer variety of forms in which the tiles were produced makes it easy to create designs that contrast with one another. Here Izue has used the key decorative piece from the apex of a gable end – a demonic face.

From inside the guest bedroom, the stand of bamboo is seen through a curtain of chains. Izue chose chains for their shimmering, waterfall-like effect, and he specified that they should be of stainless steel because it remains bright and clean.

The plan reveals the way in which buildings and several different small garden areas interlock – a design adopted to stimulate visual interest and the wish to explore. At the bottom right is the main entrance, reached by crossing a small bridge spanning a stream. The circular guest bedroom is seen in the upper right of the drawing.

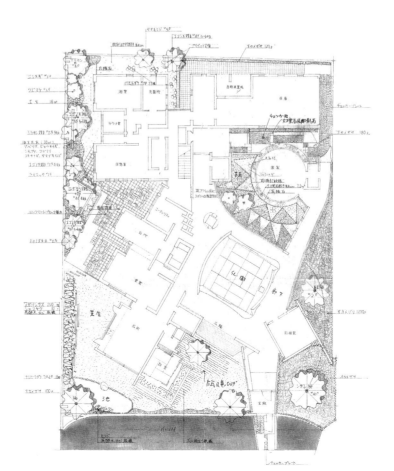

This may look like a traditional Japanese *tatami* room,
but the wall design is quite original, and was devised
purely to control and reveal views of the garden.
Although shutters can be opened and closed across
all three levels, and the upper and lower screens are
moveable, the panel on the central level is fixed,
making a complete view of the camellia impossible.

views of a curved space
design: yasujirou aoki and chitoshi kihara

Curved concrete walls in this house in Mihara, near Osaka, not only direct the sinuous path through an entrance garden that spills out onto the street, but also enclose a highly ordered garden space in which the viewing experience is tightly controlled. Curved walls are not traditional in Japanese gardens, where the right angle dominates. Günter Nitschke, Director of the Institute for East Asian Architecture and Urbanism in Kyoto, argues that the common motif underlying the Japanese garden is the superimposition of man-made perfection on nature, a combination of two types of beauty, distilled to the randomness of natural form and the severe geometry of the right angle.

In Japan the man-made crafting of nature into gardens relies heavily on the enclosed setting, and in particular on the backdrop and the frame. Such linear backdrops as the walls of the dry-stone garden at Ryoan-ji temple in Kyoto offer a deliberately strong contrast with natural form, but, in this house, architect Chitoshi Kihara wanted to create a gentler and more ambiguous setting. The principal garden, though small, is the strong focus of attention, in the shape of a quadrant of a circle, with a curved outer wall when seen from the house. The curving lines also make an interesting interplay with the strict rectangular framing provided by the picture window of the living room.

Kihara worked closely with Yasujirou Aoki, who designed the garden, as he has a number of times before and since. The theme here is control of view, by means of hints, suggestions, partial openings, and the route that starts at the street entrance and continues through two rooms: the principal living room, with its picture window, and the large tea-ceremony room. At the street entrance, just before the gate, a low, vertically slatted window in the curved wall at the left gives a restricted glimpse of the small garden inside – just enough to whet the appetite.

Inside the gate Aoki planted a *tendaiuyaku* tree (*Lindera strychnifolia*), a symbol of longevity and, by association, of doctors (the owner of the house has a medical practice).

The curved wall that encloses the principal garden also offers a small space for planting on the outside, near the street. The idea of making a *genkan-niwa*, a small exterior garden near the entrance to a building, is a specifically Japanese concept.

Beyond this is a small wooden shutter in the same curved wall, opening inwards. The strange proportions of this opening, which is half door, half window, are a reference to the tiny door that gives access to a tea-ceremony room – the "wriggling-in entrance."

　　Once in the house, the visitor finally has a perfectly staged view of the garden and its central feature, a seventy-year-old type of camellia (*Camellia wabisuke*), valued for its small, white flowers, which are no larger than 2cm (¾in) and bloom in winter. This is set on a comma-shaped mound of black peat, surrounded by a bed of small pebbles that covers the remainder of the garden. The mound echoes the curve of the wall, while its deep tone makes a striking contrast with the fallen white flowers. Instead of white sand, which would be a more usual covering, Aoki selected small, brownish pebbles, both for their softer colour and because they would help to keep the temperature of the soil underneath stable.

　　Three other plantings deliberately invoke a perspective effect, which in turn helps to exaggerate the curve of the wall. Aoki's principle was to exaggerate the sense of depth experienced when one sees the garden from the picture window, by using plants that have leaves of different size. The leaves diminish in size from those of the Japanese aralia

◡
The full view of the garden is gained from the modern living room, by using the picture window. Adding slightly to the planting a year after it was finished, Aoki placed a large-leafed Japanese aralia next to the window and a small-leafed box tree in the far corner to add to the sense of depth by including an optical illusion. The eye tends to read the leaves as being of similar size and therefore sees the trees as being further apart than they really are.

☾
In the drainage trough running between the entrance path and the wall, an almost spherical granite rock staunches the "flow" of green, river-worn pebbles. Imaginative little touches such as this are typical of the designer's work.

(*Fatsia japonica*), in the foreground, right next to the window, to the perennial *Farfugium japonicum*, surrounding the base of the camellia, and the common box tree (*Buxus microphylla*), close to the far wall.

A door on the other side of the living room admits guests to the oversized tea-ceremony room. A non-traditional arrangement of *shoji* screens on three levels gives onto the garden and the camellia. But there is a surprise. The sliding screens are so arranged that a complete view of the camellia is impossible – only a series of partial views may be enjoyed. This control is deliberate on the part of Aoki and Kihara, who wanted people to "enjoy an after-image" of the tree that they had already seen from a different angle.

Nevertheless, although the view is restricted, the tree remains the centre of attention, and, in fact, it has a special relationship with the tea ceremony. The Shogun Hideyoshi Toyotomi (1536–98) reputedly brought this species back with him from a campaign in Korea, and Sen-no-Rikyu, who perfected the tea ceremony, developed a particular affection for it – hence its name, which refers to the *wabi* concept (sometimes translated as "poverty" or "restraint") inherent in the ceremony. Indeed the tree's flowers are used for the special, restrained style of arrangement that characterizes the ritual.

wave garden
design: shunmyo masuno

Completed in 2001, after four years of work, the garden for the new Cerulean Tower Tokyu Hotel in Shibuya is regarded as one of Shunmyo Masuno's most powerful representations of landscape. Spanning the huge curve of the tall window of the lobby and lounge area, it is dominated by undulating waves of white, craggily hewn granite alternating with moss and gravel. Indeed the concept of the garden is of waves, rolling against the hotel "shore," all executed in the language of *karesansui*, the dry-stone garden (see pages 18–21).

As in Masuno's other Zen gardens designed for public spaces, the objective is to calm the mind, a task made all the more important by this hotel's location close to the insanely busy Shibuya junction, where five railways lines, one of the city's main shopping streets, and the Metropolitan Expressway all intersect. He calls the garden Kanza-tei – "sitting in tranquillity" – an allusion to a Zen phrase, *Kanza-shoufu wo kiku*, meaning "Sitting with a calm mind one can hear the sound of pine trees moving in the breeze."

The key components are terraces of white granite, which are intended to represent ocean waves, and here these terraces, more than in almost any other of his gardens, reveal the hand of the mason, many of them edged with the wedging grooves used to split them. One of Masuno's innovations in Zen gardening is hewn rocks. Traditionally, stones were taken as they were found, with great care being taken over their attitude and siting, but they were not altered. In the Momoyama period (1573–1603), stoneworking had been introduced in the form of water basins, stepping stones, and the stone *toro* lanterns, but at that time cutting had a purely functional purpose.

It was not until well after World War II that hewn rocks began to find their place in sculptural compositions in gardens. The plazas, entrances, and courtyards of public

❯❯
The principal feature of the garden, which extends in a narrow strip around the curved lobby and lounge area of the hotel (out of view to the right), is the curving terrace of pale granite ledges. These symbolize waves rolling onto a shore, which is represented here by a "beach" of stones and boulders. Concealed lighting, installed at ground level, exaggerates the lines of these ledges.

❯
Some of the large stones brought to this garden were laboriously hollowed out at the bottom to reduce their weight and so lighten the load on the building's structure. One of them had a depression at the top, which inspired Masuno to upturn it and create what looks like a natural rock arch.

♥♥

To the left of the granite "waves" is a fine old pine tree, carefully placed to provide the principal view for guests entering the hotel lobby from the street. Bands of granite and moss are arranged in layers, and conceal a sunken footpath that passes in front of the three uppermost ledges.

♥

A large basin of black granite sits in the centre of the lobby, a receptacle for a seasonally changing flower arrangement, which here is the spring design. The feature was conceived to be part of guests' experience of the garden beyond the window.

buildings, government offices, company headquarters, and large, Western-style hotels were a new kind of space for gardens, and stone lent itself particularly well to these highly focused areas of display. Its main advantages are that it can be treated as a form of sculpture; it can be given the strength of form to make a sufficient impact in relation to large-scale modern architecture; and it needs minimal maintenance. Early examples include Kenzo Tange's pond and stone garden for the Kagawa Prefectural Government offices of 1958 and sculptor Masayuki Nagare's waterfall for the Palace Hotel, Tokyo, of 1961, featuring rocks carved to form rectangles.

With stone being fashioned in this way, sculpting ideas and techniques from the world of art began to make an impact on garden design, or at least on these components. Probably the most influential of sculptors in this respect has been Isamu Noguchi (1904–88), not only because of his deep understanding of stone and skill at combining worked and unworked surfaces, but because of his vision of the place of stone in gardens and of the place of gardens in society. In his book *The Road I Have Walked* he wrote, "I think my madness in wanting to make gardens and so forth lies in this usefulness; it's a kind of humanizing of space and humanizing sculpture. It's not merely sculpture for aesthetic purposes...Rather, it is something that is actually very useful, and very much a part of people's lives. If I might say so, I think this probably comes from my own background; the need to feel that there is some place on the earth which an artist can affect in such a way that the art in that place makes for the better life and a better possibility of survival."

We already see here the beginnings of a spiritual argument for the fashioning of stone, though it is by no means always followed by other sculptors-as-gardeners. In Shunmyo Masuno's case, it is a means of expression for furthering the Zen purpose of his gardens – to aid self-awareness. As he says, "Zen gardens should be at one with the people who view them and an unforgettable garden is one that becomes an essential part of a person's life."

A key collaborator in Masuno's journey through modern Zen garden design is the stonemason Masatoshi Izumi, who has also collaborated closely with Noguchi. He writes, "Some quarried stone which bears the mark of human intervention is now being used in gardens, a tendency that is no doubt linked to the desire even within the discipline of landscape gardening to conserve nature. But this in turn is the source of an almost indescribable sense of wonderment when new forms and qualities of surfaces are exposed to the air and eye for the first time from within a large split boulder, which was perhaps so heavy that it had to be blasted from its natural lodging." Just such an occurrence, revealing an arch, is displayed here in one massive piece that is used to divide the waves of white granite from a terrace that carries the principal pine tree.

The view from the interior is always paramount, and this pine plays a role in one carefully controlled line of sight. A visitor entering the hotel lobby from outside sees, directly ahead, a massive, split-rock flower basin by Masuno – the main *objet d'art* of the lobby. Directly beyond that, seen through the window, stands the pine on its mossy mound, and beyond that again is a terrace of granite ledges that represent a waterfall. These ledges actually lie beyond a public pathway that meanders behind the plantings, and so they have a valuable added distance. To the left of this arrangement the garden changes once again to provide a different view for people in the coffee shop; what they see are almost horizontal planes of dark granite that have been worked to produce a variety of surfaces, ranging from polished to chiselled.

Laid out on a gentle slope in front of the coffee shop there is a rock garden built mainly with a granite darker than that used to represent the "waves." The surfaces of some of the stones are chiselled, while others are polished. A circle carved into the largest of the paler standing stones represents the sun.

balcony art
design: tsuyoshi nagasaki

On two small adjacent balconies in an apartment block in the residential district of Azabu, Tokyo, artist and gardener Tsuyoshi Nagasaki has created miniature gardens solely for viewing – installations that are as much works of art as gardens. Like Kazumasa Ohira (see pages 116–19), Nagasaki moves easily between garden design and other art forms. After graduating in painting from Tokyo's Geijitsu University, he moved to Spain and began working in woodcuts. This stimulated an interest in trees and, from there, in gardens.

The two commissions followed closely – as he worked on the first, the neighbour asked him to devise a treatment for her balcony space. Both are the same size, just 1m x 3m (3ft x 10ft), enclosed on the apartment side by floor-to-ceiling glass. Arguing that this was an insufficient space for actual use, Nagasaki created two tiny display gardens. Indeed, the glass enclosure has the feeling of a presentation case. A precondition for both gardens was that they could not be filled with earth, owing to the building's regulations.

In the first garden he relied on dried, cut black bamboo from Chiba prefecture, to give the impression of nature, deliberately dispensing with any greenery. This species is quite popular in Japan for fencing, but is typically tied into bunches. Nagasaki wanted a softer, indefinite presentation, and so tied the culms in layers, "planted" in a bed of white pebbles, beyond decking of pale wood. His idea for this miniature space was to give "the effect of a miniature forest, standing in snow." The layering of the bamboo creates a mysterious depth, especially at night.

The pebbles are *shironachi*, a special variety from Wakayama prefecture, known for the purity of their whiteness, and for this reason they are used as the white stones in the

Although carefully planted, these culms of black bamboo (*Phyllostachys nigra*) are, in fact, cut and dried. More often used for fencing, they are here employed by the designer as a metaphor of dark trees in snow. The pebbles, which represent the snow, were carefully chosen for their pure whiteness.

At one end of one of the balconies, culms of black bamboo were interspersed with those of a paler species to make a fence. This simple variation in tone lends visual interest to what otherwise would have been a commonplace construction.

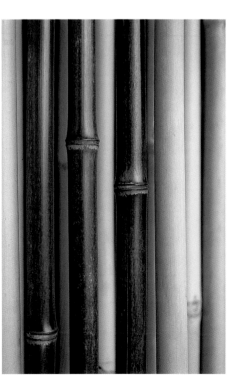

The daughter of the family for whom Nagasaki designed this balcony, christened it their "fantasy garden," because it creates an impression of a strange miniature landscape. Although none of the elements in the garden is living, its appearance changes sufficiently with the time of day to give a feeling of nature; this effect is further heightened at night, in artificial lighting provided by cubic glass lights devised by the designer.

Each element is integrated into the design of the
second balcony. The maple has been trained and
pruned to match the vertical and horizontal geometry,
and part of the inner layer of the bamboo fence has
been cut away to frame the tree's sideways spread.

traditional Japanese board game Go, which is similar to chess. As Nagasaki explains, most *shironachi* are now imported from Taiwan, but these tend to discolour to yellow, and, with his customarily meticulous approach, he insisted on this variety.

The cubic glass lights used on the two balconies are themselves works of art, devised by Nagasaki. A mould of iron was made, and a couple of pebbles were placed inside it. This was given to a glass-artist friend, who adapted the usual glass-blowing technique. First he heated the globule of glass at the end of a pipe until it was molten and then placed it inside the iron cube. When he blew the glass, it took its form from the cube but also showed oval depressions produced by the pebbles.

In designing the second balcony garden, Nagasaki took a more sculptural approach after consulting with the owner, who wanted a garden suitable for viewing the moon. Nagasaki decided on a surface that would be light and would, in an abstract, non-specific way, evoke the sky. He chose a white granite from Korea, and cut it into small, square blocks that would be the basis of a chequerboard pattern – *ichimatsu* in Japanese. He left some blocks flat, and alternated these with others that he carved to an irregular, bumpy surface in the *kobudashi* style, a traditional technique used in building stone walls, alluding to floating clouds. To maintain a feeling of softness and nature – and to add what he considers a note of melancholy – he arranged the chequerboard of bumpy blocks to dissipate from right to left. This echoes the treatment of the stone-in-moss chequerboard pattern at Tofuku-ji temple in Tokyo, re-designed by Mirei Shigemori after a fire in 1940.

At the side where the bumpy blocks have all but disappeared, Nagasaki placed a potted Japanese maple (*Acer palmatum*) for balance, as this tree is known for its relatively large leaves. The backdrop for all this is his own design of bamboo fence. The species of bamboo, *Arundinaria japonica*, is known for its small diameter, and Nagasaki arranged it horizontally, tying it not with the normal black cord but with wisteria tendrils soaked for a couple of hours in water. In the surface of the granite he embedded cubic glass lights blown in the same way as those used next door; the difference here is that the upper surface of each cube carries an impression of a piece of granite inserted into the mould.

Exquisite attention to detail has been put into the balcony gardens, despite the fact that they are too small for practical use, as this view from inside one of the apartments shows. The rectangular frame created by the glass wall reinforces the sense that the space is intended to be seen as an art installation.

On the second balcony Nagasaki installed cubic glass lights, textured by the use of granite in an iron mould. The granite forming the floor of the terrace has been cut away so that the hollow cubes could be inserted, and the wiring has been run beneath the blocks of stone.

a hand-crafted patio
design: tsuyoshi nagasaki

Among Tsuyoshi Nagasaki's meticulous creations, and occupying only a little more space than the two balcony gardens in Azabu (see pages 110–13), is this patio garden for a small family living in Kichijouji, a pleasant suburb of Tokyo. The area available was on a narrow street in front of the house, but, in this neighbourly area, which has a large park close by, privacy was not a concern. Rather, the clients wanted a space that would be a suitable play area for the family's two young children. A second condition was that the persimmon tree (*Diospyros kaki*) already standing in front of the house should not be cut down. The owner comes from a line of Shinto priests and, for religious reasons, could not countenance such destruction of nature.

Nagasaki decided on a pale theme, and selected the materials and plants accordingly. He prefers to do everything himself, and set about constructing the decking and fencing around the persimmon. As the patio was likely to receive heavy use by the children, he restricted the plantings to the perimeter. At the same time he designed the fencing so that it would give views of the plants and of the patinated copper lamps, which were, in fact, made in the United States but are intended as an interpretation of the traditional Japanese *toro* stone lantern. The plan is that when the children are older the fencing and decking will be removed, and the planted garden extended, but, for the time being, the planting is concentrated in a curved bed around the patio.

The low wall for the bed is built with a white, weathered brick from Australia, which Nagasaki also used to pave the entrance adjacent to the patio, where he additionally included small, recycled Spanish tiles. Bricklaying is not a traditional skill in Japan, and so, for the paving at the entrance, he himself laid the bricks, in a chequerboard pattern. To add structural interest to the wall and make a sharp contrast to the pale bricks, he brought in black volcanic boulders and cut the bricks to fit into them.

The persimmon, a very traditional Japanese tree because of its fruit, is typically very leafy – too much so for this location. The Japanese gardening term is *komu*, meaning "crowded," and the usual trimming method is to cut some of the branches. On aesthetic grounds, however, Nagasaki preferred the more laborious technique of thinning out the leaves to keep the shape of the branches. But, because the patio faces south-east, a second tree was needed to provide summer shade, and for this he chose a crepe myrtle (*Lagerstroemia indica*). The attractive features of this tree, imported from southern China during the Edo period, are its smooth, slippery, reddish bark and its white flowers. (There is a red variety, but Nagasaki wanted to continue the pale theme for the garden.) Wood from the same tree is used for the gate handle.

At the rear of the house, he constructed a path of square concrete stepping stones, some of which are set with shells and glass marbles collected by the children, while others carry impressions of a fern and the family's handprints.

This stepping stone behind the house was decorated by the whole family, who placed their hands on the concrete while it was still wet. Other stones in the path contain decorative items chosen by the children.

This shows the patio garden from the street in front of the house. When they are no longer needed to form a children's play area, the fencing and decking, made by the designer, will give way to additional plantings.

While Nagasaki aimed to achieve a subtle collection of colours – and for this reason avoided bright flowering plants – he wanted to experiment with contrasts of tone and shape. With this in mind, he juxtaposed pale, weathered brick and the pitted, organic form of dark volcanic boulders from Oshima.

In the original sketch for the patio and the adjacent driveway, the project's essential appearance was already established. Among the changes Nagasaki introduced later was a fence, to increase privacy, and the use of lower plants behind the low brick wall.

The arrangement of the stepping stones responds to the garden's near-rectangular space, and, by branching off towards the area between the pine and the maple, the path creates a focal point between the two opposed trees.

art installation

design: kazumasa ohira

Entitled "Abstraction Garden" by its designer, this arrangement of stones on gravel, flanked by two opposing trees, is a study in focused composition. At the centre is a ceramic water vessel, smaller than the other elements, but ultimately the strongest feature.

The designer is the highly regarded sculptor and potter Kazumasa Ohira. Initially trained as a landscape gardener, he has no conceptual difficulty in combining the arts of garden design and ceramics (an example of the way in which, in Japan, garden design is accorded the same respect as other fields of art). The family that owns this property in the town of Kibugawa, near Lake Biwa, run a business manufacturing the wooden boxes used for quality ceramics, which is how they came to know Ohira, whose workshop and kilns are in the wooded hills a short drive away. When the time came to redesign the old garden, they already knew whom to ask.

Ohira saw the project as part garden, part installation. His current work is almost entirely in clay, but he uses it as he has used metal and stone in his environmental sculptures. His ceramics have a characteristic rock-like quality (and surprise many people touching them for the first time, who believe them to be stone), which he has achieved by intense experimentation with local Shigaraki and Iga clays. He doctors the clay by first washing it thoroughly to rid it of impurities and then mixing it with feldspar and silica. He goes a step further in the direction of stone with his robust treatment of the clay, making pieces as heavy and thick as possible – typically 5cm (2in). This involves long drying periods (several months for large pieces) and a single firing. The result is a strong body of work that is intended materially and visually to sit in the environment alongside natural features, and indeed Ohira's preferred method of display is in nature.

A ceramic container, one of the artist's "Water Vessel" series, occupies the focal point of the garden at the termination of one arm of the stepping stones. It works well in this position because the technique used for making these pieces gives them the appearance of carved stone.

This early plan proposed that the stepping stones should enclose the water vessel in a fork, but this idea was later abandoned. Now, although their ostensible purpose is to create a path from the side entrance on the left to the tiled main entrance to the house on the right, the stones also form a pattern for the eye.

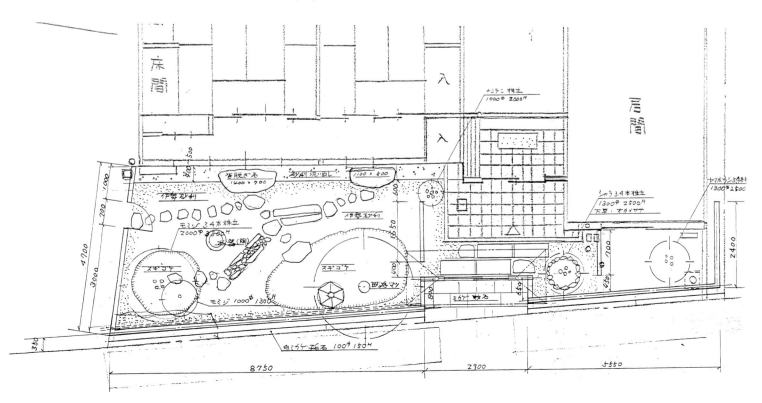

☾

Although it would have been easy to give a full view of the garden to a visitor approaching the front door, the designer chose instead to give a less obvious, more intriguing view by erecting a free-standing wall (above left). Here, the gate leading to the garden is open, but, even when it is closed, there remains a truncated view of the black pine. Stepping up to the gap in the wall (above right) reveals a little more, as intended. The principle of the incomplete view is a part of traditional Japanese garden design.

☾

At the rear of the house, behind a glass wall that spans the width of the main corridor, is a tiny, pebble-strewn garden. Within this space, sheltered by two side walls and a backdrop of galvanized-iron sheets, another of the artist's ceramic works is displayed. The angles to which the metal sheets are cut reflect the jagged rim of the ceramic.

The piece Ohira chose for this garden was one of a recent series that he calls "Water Vessels" (*Mizuki*), occupying a place roughly between bowls and the stone water basins typical of traditional gardens. These are not vessels for practical use, however, but for displaying water. Their rough texture recalls the nearby craggy Iga mountains, and the water contained symbolizes mountain pools and rainwater, so that each of the *Mizuki* is another statement of the old Japanese garden obsession with mountains and water.

A given element in the garden was the fifty-year-old pine tree in one corner, an attractive specimen that the family wanted to keep. This is a Japanese black pine (*Pinus thunbergii*), named for its black bark, which has a texture likened by Japanese gardeners to a turtle's shell. Ohira balanced this with a second tree, and, in recognition of the black pine's strongly masculine appearance, he chose for the other corner a maple to represent femininity. In this way he introduced a balance and the opposition of yin and yang, to be resolved somewhere in between with his water vessel.

As the surface of the garden would be covered with tiny pebbles, Ohira sharpened the trees' sculptural qualities by surrounding each with a mound of deep-green hair-cap moss (*Polytrichum juniperinum*), which grows to 10cm (4in). "I made two islands: one strong, one soft," he says.

There are three entrances to the rectangular garden: a small gate at each end and the door of a *tatami* room in the middle of one long side. To cross the sea of pebbles, Ohira arranged stepping stones that meander from one gate to the other, connecting with the principal stone in front of the *tatami*-room – the *kutsunugi-ishi*, or "stone for removing shoes." He specifically selected these stones for their reddish-brown colour – the Japanese name means "rust stone." On their way across the garden, the stepping stones make a half detour, and at this point a flat rectangle of smaller stones set in concrete heads off diagonally. Beyond this, out of the way and yet clearly the focus of the entire arrangement, is the water vessel, its internally rippled surface suggesting movement in the still liquid.

A second ceramic piece by Ohira can be seen at the rear of the house, in a tiny garden at the end of the main corridor. Viewed through a tall sheet of glass, it sits on a bed of pebbles, with a backdrop provided by a sheet of galvanized iron divided into irregular sections. The iconic presentation is deliberate, as this small space, lit by daylight from above, represents a *tokonoma*, an alcove in a tea-ceremony room.

glass and water
design: kengo kuma

On its completion in 1998 the spectacular Water/Glass House designed by Kengo Kuma drew widespread acclaim for its imaginative, illusory use of transparency and reflection. In a variety of projects in recent years Kuma has gained a reputation for his exploration of the subtle qualities of different materials. He also designed the Stone Plaza in Tochigi prefecture (see pages 126–9). But here, for a relatively large residential commission – a three-storey villa in the seaside resort of Atami – he worked mainly with glass and steel.

Kuma's aim was to create transparency, translucency, and reflection, combining the effects of water and glass, as the name he gave the villa indicates. The site, high on one of the two headlands that enclose the bay of this historic resort, suggested the theme. It has a 270° panoramic view, mainly over the Pacific Ocean, and Kuma exploited this by cantilevering a large block of granite out from the top floor and turning it into a kind of infinity pool, with water trickling over the edge. On this floor there are mirror-like views from the main bedroom, the living room, and the dramatic dining room, the last encased in an oval of glass, and set like an island in the pool. The shallow water seems to merge with the ocean beyond, and, as Kuma says, "There is no edge to the water. Just the water itself." An enclosed path leads diagonally out to the dining room in reference to the stage in Noh theatre, which is traditionally surrounded by a bare, empty garden.

Below, at ground level, Kuma wanted to continue the interplay of reflection and transparency in a garden that would enter the house from outside. One limitation here was that the land area was just a 3m (10ft) wide strip in front of the house; the roof of the

‹
For one or two hours early in the morning, if the sky is clear, the optical glass of these boulders acts like a prism. The rocks create a shifting play of light, modulated by the water in the pond, on the wall behind them.

‹ ‹
Glass rocks are clustered in the outer half of a shallow pool, opposite a large *tatami* room. This room, though enclosed in glass, has sliding screens that open onto a view dominated by the rocks. By etching some of the surfaces at an intermediate stage in the cutting, the glass artist was able to simulate the half-hewn, half-natural effect in stone carving pioneered by Isamu Noguchi, the sculptor who has possibly had the greatest influence on the modern Japanese use of rocks in the garden.

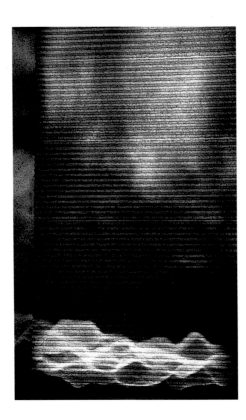

The top floor, two storeys above the pool with glass rocks, is cantilevered out to create a black-granite infinity pool that overflows at the edge and merges visually with the Pacific beyond.

neighbouring property on the downslope side also prevented an infinite view similar to the one on the top floor. Here, for privacy, Kuma planted a dense, bushy, evergreen *Skimmia japonica*. The principal interior at this level is a large *tatami* room for entertaining, enclosed in glass but with sliding screens as well. The garden enters along one side of this room.

Kuma's idea here was to create a large interior pool which would be connected to the exterior by a channel and a three-storey atrium above. The main entrance to the house is reached by crossing a bridge set one level above the pool, and on the house side of the bridge he planned a textured concrete wall down which water would flow the full height of the building. He also envisaged a glass feature within the pool, to extend the concept of the house, but at this stage he had nothing specific in mind.

At the gallery of an *ikebana*, or flower-arranging, society, Kuma met Tomohiro Kano, a glass artist whose work was being featured, and the architect immediately realized that Kano had the answer. By this time the Water/Glass House had been completed, and when the artist visited the site he saw that he would have to accommodate the strict geometry of the pool and walkways. "This was architecture of very sharp straight lines, and a similar treatment to the glass would compete with it," he explained. In addition he was concerned not to obstruct the lines of the pond except, as he put it, "with light reflections and shadow." The answer, which was straightforward yet original, was to fashion boulders from glass. Their "natural" lines would harmonize with the right angles of the pond in just the same way that the natural rock formations in a traditional Zen garden interact with the man-made geometry of the enclosing walls.

With this in mind, Kano decided to work the glass like a stonemason. He ordered a large block of optical glass, for its high refractivity, from a company that supplies lens makers. Its dimensions were 3m x 3m x 1.5m (10ft x 10ft x 5ft), and from this he carved out a group of glass rocks with a hammer and chisel. The garden faces east, and when the sun clears the bushes it strikes the "stones," which illuminate, refracting light around the pool. Movements in the water, from a breeze or from the vertical waterfall, add to this effect, and harmonic patterns play over the walls. To increase the interest and variety of this natural light show, Kano also etched some of the faces of the boulders.

◡

A second group of glass rocks, placed at the end of the channel that connects the lower pool to the exterior of the house, softens the angular lines and leads the eye between the outside and inside, as can be seen in the overall view on pages 124–25.

◖ ◗

Blue underwater lights are positioned at the foot of the three-storey vertical wall that occupies one side of the atrium. The ribbed surface of the concrete wall breaks up the water that falls in a shimmering cascade from the top of this space.

◖ ◖

The tatami room is enclosed in glass, but has sliding screens that open to give a tranquil interior view dominated by the pile of glass rocks in the pool.

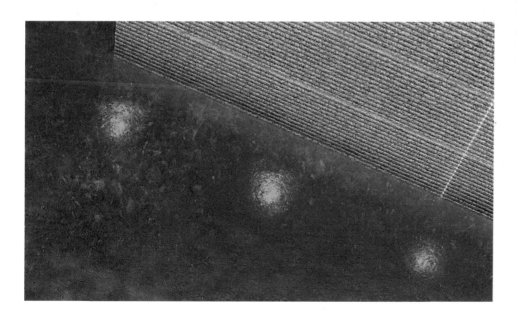

stone reflections
design: kengo kuma

Built between 1996 and 2000, Stone Plaza in Tochigi prefecture, north of Tokyo, is a museum space commissioned by a company that deals in the local Ashino and Shirakawa stones – both varieties of andesite (formed at the time of eruption of nearby Mount Nasu). Kengo Kuma was the architect, and his brief stressed two main points: to demonstrate new uses for the stone, and to use it in a soft and light manner. The site chosen, acquired from the local rice association, contained stone warehouses that dated from the beginning of the twentieth century. In a sense the entire site is the museum.

Kuma's primary task, as he defined it, was to add "soft" walls in a counterpoint to the existing "hard" stone architecture of the old warehouses. He achieved this by means of a slatted construction in which the stone was sliced into thin, 4cm (1½in), slabs, separated vertically by the same distance, and by an arrangement of thicker slabs laid with openings at regular intervals. Kuma calls the effect "vibration," adding that "Japanese architecture is often called lightweight architecture, but this is a mistake. Japanese architecture vibrates. It vibrates between existence and expression."

The treatment of the exterior space was of great importance. Kuma wanted an effect similar to that of the Shinto temples at the Imperial Shrine at Isé. There, the wooden structures rise over grounds of round, white stones, which are, he says, "wonderfully light… At times they function as a solid stone foundation. At other times they seem to drift like particles of light." Here, a traditional garden would be inappropriate because it would distract attention from the stone. What was needed was a surface that would have the Isé "vibration," and Kuma chose to make the garden with the simplest, purest combination – stone pathways and water. As we have already seen in a number of other gardens, stone is as much a part of the vocabulary of Japanese gardening as are plants, and while a plantless garden might seem extreme in a Western context, it is perfectly rational in Japan. Kuma wanted to achieve "this kind of wavering between existence and expression" with the pale, textured local andesite, complementing it with water, in shallow, geometric ponds that would themselves look like soft, reflecting slabs. By giving each pond a bed of blackened andesite chips, and adding underwater uplighters along the edges, he provided a visible texture that recalls the surface of the stone.

With the geometry of planes replacing grass, trees, and rocks, this is a modern version of a "stroll garden," one of the traditional forms imported from China. It is directly inspired by the famous garden of the seventeenth-century Imperial Katsura Villa in Kyoto, in which the path provides constant changes of view and a rhythmic feeling of tension.

The shallow pools of water that alternate with the paths function as a display space for sculptures in an exhibition that changes periodically. These works, by the artist Mitsuo Kikuchi, benefit from reflections that reveal their undersides.

The garden of stone and water also had to serve as a means for directing visitors around the museum site. The paths intersect the ponds at a variety of angles, and, except for the one at the far end, cannot be crossed from one to another. Instead they form a kind of zigzag route that leads through stone corridors and a small plaza. This arrangement consciously recalls the circuitous routes found in some traditional temple gardens, which lead the visitor to specific points from where there are different views – the *tachidomaru* spots at which to "pause, stop, look." This is a technique not only for organizing the museum display, but also for enlarging the space experientially. Seen from the road at the front, the site is deliberately open, bordered by just a low stone ledge. The water bounds the plaza, like a moat, and one pathway crosses it to reach the old warehouse that serves as the museum entrance and reception. From this building, one pathway emerges like a jetty, leading nowhere but provided with simple seating and a ledge for resting. A second pathway leads diagonally from one corner across the water to a stone-walled corridor, which delivers the visitor to a new view and another path crossing to the plaza. A third and a fourth path continue the route.

The pale grey of the stone itself reflects the colour of the changing light, and this feature is enhanced by the even more reflective, even softer, surfaces of the water. The pathways are raised just a little above the ponds, so that to walk around the garden is to experience a feeling of lightness. After a shower, these paths reflect the sky and buildings almost as completely as the ponds do, and the play of intersecting lines between the horizontals of the walls, the verticals of the building corners, and the diagonals of the pathways, becomes even more interesting and ambiguous.

The water garden and buildings are completely open to the main street of the small town of Ashino, once one of the main trunk roads of the Edo period, but the water is an effective barrier. The two century-old warehouses are at right and in the distance, connected by modern paths and buildings made of the local pale-grey andesite.

The garden is organized into a number of key views that present themselves suddenly as the visitor turns a corner or, as here, emerges from a doorway in the enclosed corridor that runs the length of the southern side of the garden.

For the long wall on the south side of the garden, Kuma used a "light" construction, in which thin slabs are laid horizontally and equally spaced. Uplighters, submerged in the ponds in a row just in front of the wall, add visual interest to the design.

path to simplicity
design: yasujirou aoki, chitoshi kihara, and masa tada

The space available for this city garden in Osaka is a moderately steep slope rising from the entrance to a level area some 2.5m (8ft) above. At the foot of the path, the garden is dark and green, but, as the path climbs, the colours brighten until the tea-ceremony room at the top is reached. This looks out onto a minimally designed bed of pebbles containing a single plant. The designer of the garden, Yasujirou Aoki, working with architects Chitoshi Kihara and Masa Tada (Aoki's wife), organized the path and the planting to take into account lines of sight on both the ascent and descent.

The planting was the main means by which Aoki created distinctive views at these two stages. However, the space was wide enough to allow him to slightly turn the stone steps in places, and he achieved changes of line of sight in this way too. (He would have made the steps turn more, but he was restricted by the fact that they had to be wide enough to accommodate the wheelchair of the owner's grandfather when he visited.) Aoki made sure that the key plants and assemblies of plants acknowledged these turns. At the first, for example, a flowering dogwood (*Cornus florida*) on one side faces a *Rhododendron yakushimanum* on the other. At the very sharp turn above this, against a stone wall, Aoki planted a group of three Japanese juneberry trees (*Amelanchier asiatica*), with a climber (*tsurumono*) and shrubs. At the top, the main eye-catcher is a hybrid of *Magnolia kobus*, known as Wada's Memory, with abundant, white flowers.

The key to Aoki's method of varying the view is that he follows the principles of *ikebana*, or Japanese flower arrangement. Despite the existence of different *ikebana* schools, each with its own particular style, there is one concept that is basic to all. This, deriving from the Three Worlds of Buddhism, is the tripartite arrangement of elements and the three-dimensional variation of the arrangement when seen from different angles. A typical tripartite arrangement in *ikebana* is a tall, vertical element, a lower, falling element,

A single plant, an iris, occupies the upper level of the garden, set in an old stone horse trough that is itself a circle within a circle. This stark simplicity, and the only hint of green among the shades of grey of the pebble pond, contrasts strikingly with the plants that fill the slope below. The *shoji* screens on the left are those of the tea-ceremony room.

The principles of *ikebana* flower arrangement are here put to use around a red-leafed *Loropetalum chinense* f. *rubrum* to make a dynamic, three-tiered arrangement offering views that range from upslope to downslope.

In the pebble pond the crescent motif, surrounding the plant pot, was created simply by clearing a space among the loose pebbles to reveal the concrete base of the pond. In the spring, cherry blossoms overhang the surface of the water.

and a diagonal element in the middle. Aoki's garden version of this principle is exemplified by three clusters to the right of the path, each situated around a hornbeam. Chosen for their lack of prominent flowers, the hornbeams are the main vertical element; at the base of each of these are rocks and low perennials, while the central diagonal element is flowering shrubs.

Indoor flower arrangements in Japan are usually set against a background, which limits the directions from which they can be viewed to less than 180 degrees. Even so, three-dimensionality is important in this tradition. In Aoki's garden the same restriction applies, with the wall providing the background. In the case of the hornbeams, he has positioned three different flowering shrubs in a semicircle around each tree, so that the view changes according to whether one walks up or down.

On the level space at the top of the garden, the treatment is austere by comparison. This area is designed to provide a contemplative view from the adjacent tea-ceremony room. *Shoji* screens set along the wall of the room open to give a non-traditional breadth of view. Normally, the visual focus in the tea-ceremony room would be a *kakejiku* scroll painting, typically a landscape, hanging in the *tokonoma*, or alcove. This painting would be changed with each season. As Kihara says, "In the past, decorating the *tokonoma* was an important and enjoyable activity in the home, and four times a year a different painting would evoke the new season." However, good scroll paintings are now very expensive. Moreover, the lifestyle that allows time for this formal acknowledgment of the seasons has largely disappeared from modern cities, and the architect's concession to this change was to make the exterior view perform the same function. The view through the open screens takes the place of the scroll painting, and it largely takes care of itself – with the help of occasional visits by Aoki.

In the restricted space available there was no room for the components that are normally associated with Japan's seasons, such as cherry and maple. Aoki, unperturbed, approached the task in two ways: literal and symbolically. On the literal level, he made the key focal point a plant container, adapted from an old stone horse trough from a farm, in which he could place a plant appropriate to each season. In spring 2001, for example, he planted an iris, while the previous summer he had added a papyrus. Symbolically, he created a setting that has "a change of face," as he puts it – a change that the owner can implement at will. He laid the entire rectangular surface with pebbles, except for a crescent around the plant container, adding a few more to make a small mound, which, when viewed from the tea-ceremony room, gives a visual balance to the single plant. The design recalls the pebble-strewn precincts of the Shinto Imperial Shrine at Isé.

By adding a water supply and drainage, Aoki gave the owner the ability to create a pond at will by flooding the pebbles. These play a dual visual role, and it was important to choose ones that would produce the desired effect. Aoki selected a variety called *nachiguro* from Wakayama prefecture, south of Osaka, which are pale grey when dry but a deep, shiny black when wet. The pond creates a softer impression than the bed of dry pebbles, and the small mound becomes a tiny island in the water.

The first view of the garden, from just inside the gated street entrance, takes in a stepped path that winds gently upwards past hornbeams, shadbush, dogwood, rhododendron, and other plants.

Two faces of the pebble pond – flooded and dry –
each with its own tradition in Japanese gardening.
Characteristic of the designer's work is the painterly
precision with which all the elements are organized.

❍ The white wall acts both as the centrepiece of the view from the street and separates the stone-paved driveway that leads to the upper level and the grassy path that goes down to the garden. There is no gate, and the garden is so inviting that occasionally passers-by come in and sit on the bench just inside; the owners, who have a popular local restaurant, affect not to mind.

☾ Although the wall divides the upper level of the garden from the lower level, the grading of the plot is not that simple. A steep cut was made along the line of the wall, so that the driveway climbs up to the entrance of the house, while the garden descends. The purpose of the excavation on the lower side was to maximize the extent of the white backdrop against which the trees are set.

dividing wall

design: gyoko osumi and akira sakamoto

This garden in Tondabayashi, a residential suburb of Osaka, was awarded the city's Green View prize, the Midori no Keikan sho, in 1996, and is the result of a collaboration between gardener Gyoko Osumi and architect Akira Sakamoto. The property combines two former empty plots of land on two different levels on the hillside, and this gave Sakamoto a variety of slopes with which to play.

One of the client's key demands was that there should be separate accommodation for his mother, but that this should be integrated within the complex. Sakamoto's solution was to site the main house and its garden on the lower slope – on the right as one enters the property – and the smaller building, for his mother, on the level ground above and to the left of these. The lower garden is the main focus of attention, and is designed to be seen primarily from the balcony of the living room, which looks down on it. At the same time, Osumi and Sakamoto designed it to work when seen from other viewpoints, including from a sheltered bay at the foot of the garden and from a curving stone path that runs up from this garden to the upper one.

Then, in typically Japanese fashion, Sakamoto decided to exercise a measure of control over how the main garden was approached. From the street entrance, the garden slopes down to the right, and the architect wanted to conceal part of it, so as to intrigue the visitor – the same principle as was used by Yoshiji Takehara in his dry-stone garden for a house on the slopes of Hieizan (see pages 18–21). He erected a free-standing wall, 2.5m (8ft) at its highest point and 25m (82ft) long, partly separating the driveway from the garden, and painted the wall white.

Using two techniques from *shakkei* (see pages 34–9), the wall controls the view in two ways. It partly closes off the space from outside, and, when seen from within the garden, it acts as an illusionistic backdrop. From the curving stone path, the view towards

The garden is designed to be enjoyed not only from its own level, but as a view from the balcony to the living and dining room, and for this the broad curve of the path, stepped with old wooden railway sleepers and lined with shrubs, provides a focal point. The view corresponds to the lower left part of the plan on the opposite page.

the wall is an upward one, in which wall and sky merge. Osumi planted *Magnolia kobus* trees against the wall, with their upper branches masking its top edge. As the trees are seen as silhouettes they make a strong visual impact against a white surface that at first glance seems to be the sky. This makes the garden appear larger. "I wanted," she says, "to create an illusion – that of a childhood memory of gardens, always larger than the gardens themselves." Her planting – camellia, azalea, cherry – is natural in style and needs much less maintenance than a traditional Japanese garden. The owners also enjoy gardening, and have added other plants, including ferns such as *Dryopteris crassirhizoma*, *Dryopteris erythrosora*, and the ostrich fern (*Matteuccia struthiopteris*).

For the mother's house, which is single-storey and on the upper level of the plot, Sakamoto and Osumi designed a perimeter garden that follows the lines of the rooms' inner walls, in order to fill the view from every window. From the *tatami* room, there are two views – a low one that is seen in the traditional way, from a sitting position on the floor, and a view enjoyed from standing height as one enters the room. For this second view, Sakamoto gave the room a non-traditional long opening that looks directly out onto the narrow garden, in addition to the smaller opening in the adjacent wall. The plants used in the perimeter garden are more traditional than those in the main garden, and include a variety of maples, chosen for their seasonal combinations of leaf colour, and azaleas.

Dividing the two houses and their gardens is a driveway that climbs up from the street and leads to a parking area outside the main house. Sakamoto rejected concrete as too bleak and empty for the driveway. He favoured a surface that would have a half-natural appearance and that would provide, when seen from the street entrance, a soft counterpoint to the "sharpness" of the dividing wall. In addition, he wanted to make a textured connection between not just the two gardens but also the exterior and interior of the main house. "This space is actually a modern version of the old *doma* – the earthen floor that formed the connecting space for walking between the different parts of old houses. I wanted it to be half outside, half inside." He settled on a surface of small, rounded, granite stones, which were tightly spaced, and similar to the paving at Hama Rikyu, the Imperial garden on Tokyo Bay. The owner of the house is president of a construction company and was able to obtain special *gorota-ishi* stones from Isé. Sakamoto had them set in concrete, and continued them into the hallway of the house, right up to the raised floor.

On the sketch plan the street entrance can be seen on the left, while the white wall clearly cuts the property in half horizontally.

The narrow perimeter garden is seen from the *tatami* room in the smaller house. While the *tatami* room is, in principle, traditional, the large opening on the left is not. Usually the view is through a low window, as on the right, seen from a sitting position on the floor, but this larger opening gives a view as one enters the room.

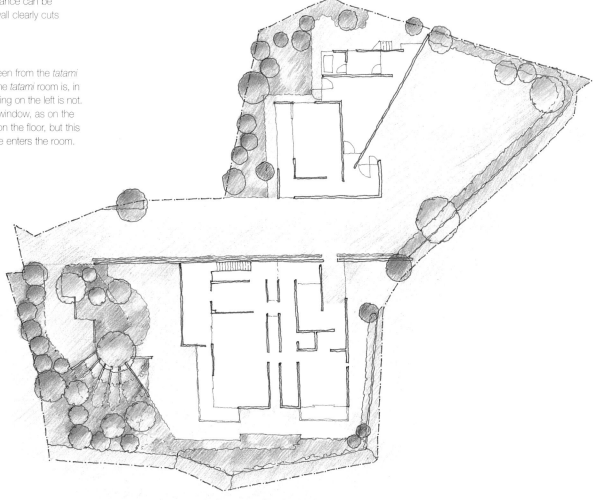

basement step garden
design: masayuki yoshida

The first view of the basement garden is gained on entering the door to the salon. A sliding window frames the garden to exclude the upper garden level. On the left is a paper lantern designed by the Japanese-American sculptor Isamu Noguchi.

As part of the spring planting, Yoshida chose an early-flowering *Astilbe* x *arendsii* 'Venus' for the topmost tier of the step garden, because of its delicate, feathery panicles. The bright-pink flowers pick up the theme established by the cherry blossoms that crown the arrangement shown on the opposite page.

Approaching the basement window reveals the upper garden level, and a surprise in spring – a *Prunus* 'Shōgetsu' cherry tree heavily laden with pink and white blossoms that face down towards the room.

In 1999 Takashi Mikuriya, a professor of political science, and his wife decided to convert their basement into a salon and small gallery in which to entertain friends who shared their interest in literature and art. Since 1994, when the house was built, this room had languished behind the parking bay as a dimly lit storage room. It was time to turn it into a useful and attractive space, and key to this was the role of the steep bank of earth that sloped down to the sliding glass doors from the garden above. The area available for a basement garden was restrictive – a sunken cube of 2.4m (8ft) in each dimension.

The couple called on the talents of gardener Masayuki Yoshida, who normally works on grander projects such as hotel and golf-club gardens. "As it is essentially underground, I needed to make this a *hikari-niwa* ['light garden'] and draw the light and plants down to this level from the upper garden," Yoshida says. He conceived a step garden composed of descending ledges that would allow a number of separate plantings. To demarcate the steps and create a strong, sculptural shape between the concrete retaining walls on either side, he chose old wooden railway sleepers; some were laid horizontally to make the ledges, while others were driven vertically into the earth, to create nine separate small areas on seven levels. "Although of wood, the form of the sleepers is much stronger than that of normal logs, and I used them in a way similar to *ishigumi* – stone composition. They had to be strong enough to match the concrete walls, and I wanted to play with a contrast of three materials. Cool, inorganic white concrete is set against powerful rustic wood aged by use, and both contrast with the delicacy and softness of the variety of plants."

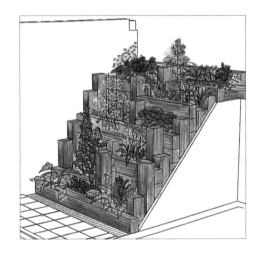

Drainage is controlled at the base by a trough fitted with a stainless-steel grid, and, to give visual definition and textural contrast with the wooden sleepers, Yoshida laid white quartzite pebbles in the trough. A reed screen helps to define the top of the step garden, and therefore its dark mass is framed by clear, light edges on all four sides: pale concrete left and right, white pebbles below, and reed screen above. The height of the plantings at the top is controlled to show the cherry tree above to its best advantage. This is particularly important for *hanami*, or "cherry-blossom viewing," in April, when the dense flowers dominate the view through the glass sliding doors of the salon. The species of cherry tree was chosen with care; called *shogetsu*, it is a variety of *yaezakura*, or "eightfold petal cherry tree." It was selected because the flowers are so heavy that they face downwards and therefore present their best aspect to this underground viewpoint. The tree blooms rather later than most cherries, in the second half of April.

In Japan the four seasons are clearly distinct, and the change from one to the next is predictable to within a few days. This differentiation has had a marked effect on the Japanese approach to nature, art, and gardening. Cherry-blossom viewing is the singular example of this, an occasion for friends to gather and picnic. Kimonos have seasonal designs, and the food displayed in both restaurants serving *kaiseki*, or high-quality, dishes and in department stores changes seasonally, as do the flower arrangements in the *tokonoma*, the alcove in a tea-ceremony room.

This step garden gives Yoshida the opportunity to make four complete changes of planting each year. In spring, pink cherry blossom sets the accent, and he uses, among other plants, hydrangea, ferns, orchids, lavenders, and rosemary. In summer, he replaces these with plants that have stronger colours, such as reds, including bellflower, hibiscus, ixora, and caladiums, all from Okinawa and Japan's southern islands. Autumn sees a change to colours that promote what Yoshida calls "calmness and composure," so the planting in October 2000 had the theme of purple. In winter, his choice of planting set up an interplay between reds including that of euphorbia and abundant green foliage. Making the most of the changing seasons in such a small space means using flowers – not a traditional practice in the Japanese garden – but Yoshida admits a fascination with English gardening. Moreover, these seasonal changes allow him to take responsibility for his creation. "While I enjoy the larger projects, we never get the chance to look after them once our work has finished. Here I can return and care for the garden."

❩

In summer, the delicate shades of spring are replaced by stronger reds, including *Ixora coccinea*, begonias, and caladium, and deeper greens, such as asplenium, *Passiflora caerulea*, vinca, and ivy.

❩

Yoshida's meticulous seasonal plans include precise drawings of how the garden will look. The garden was completed in mid-2000, and these are the four seasonal plantings for, from left to right, summer 2000, autumn 2000, winter 2000, and spring 2001.

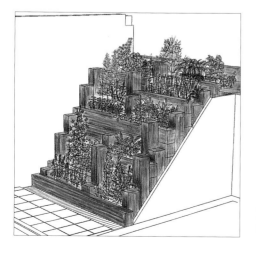 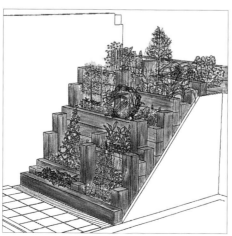 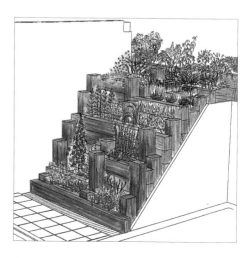

☽

Viewed from the foot of the slope that climbs to the house, the lower garden begins with a gently curving path of granite blocks leading through a landscape dotted with a mixture of bamboo species.

☾

A stand of tall, tufted Narihira bamboo (*Semiariundinaria fastuosa*) blends with the grass lining the path that leads up to the house, as well as sheltering and concealing the front door.

☾ ☾

The plan shows the lower garden on the left, connected by a narrow path on one side of the house (coloured orange) to the rear garden on the right. The curved earthen wall runs through both house and garden.

a return to nature
design: masaki tokui

Architect Masaki Tokui decided in 1999 to move back to the countryside of his native Gunma prefecture, preferring to commute by high-speed train to his Tokyo office rather than live in the city. Tokui has a close relationship with two of the other architects in this book – Kosuke Izumi (see pages 68–71) and Michimasa Kawaguchi (see pages 26–9) – and all three share similar feelings towards natural traditions, which are expressed in the muted colours and unaffected textures of earth (in the case of Izumi's Doro-outzu house) and in *sumi* ink (in Kawaguchi's courtyard garden).

The plot Tokui bought rises 9m (30ft) from the road, and he sited the house at the top, leaving plenty of space for two gardens. One covers the slope leading up to the house, and there is a smaller, enclosed garden onto which the living areas face. Central to his treatment of the two gardens, both of which have a deliberate disorder to them, was the wish to maintain a sense of natural wildness, without simply letting them run wild. Before work began, the land was covered largely by bamboo and bamboo grass, and Tokui decided to incorporate these into the plantings.

The underlying inspiration for this dwelling, the architect explains, is the nest, which in nature is usually assembled from materials gathered from the local habitat. Tokui was drawn to the idea of fixing the house and garden firmly in the locale, so that, rather than being imposed on the land, as many houses are, it would be an integral part of it. He introduced fifteen species, including the dogwood *Cornus kousa*, but there are actually more than fifty species growing here, some of which would be considered weeds. Complementing the naturalness of the gardens, the traditional Japanese *kawara* clay roof tiles are locally hand-crafted, and the earth used to clad one of the principal walls of the house and garden (shown in the large photograph overleaf) was taken from the plot itself.

The large garden that covers the approach to the house is dominated by five species of bamboo, ranging in size from large *Phyllostachys pubescens* at the foot of the steps, through the elegant Narihira bamboo (*Semiarundinaria fastuosa*) near the door, to the low ground cover of the dwarf bamboo grass (*Sasa veitchii syn. S. albomarginata*).

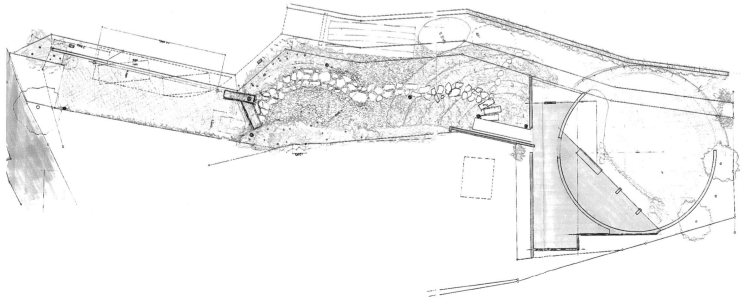

The apparently random planting – which is, in fact, carefully considered – helps to frame the view from the foot of the slope and lead the eye up the hill. Uneven trimming, particularly of the evergreen bamboo grass *Shibataea kumasasa*, reduces the impression of steepness, as does the winding path of rough granite steps.

A further expression of this "localization," or deliberate relating of the home to the habitat, was the integration of the building and the upper garden, with its dogwood and rustic benches. The wide view of the garden offered by the wooden living room suggested one way to achieve this integration. The plants come right up to the window, while the window's low height excludes the sky from the view, making a more intimate connection between room and garden.

Another device that Tokui used to create the impression that the house runs into the garden and vice versa was the curved earthen wall. This runs right through the house and out on both sides, sloping down on the right to lead the eye through the windows and back out into the garden. The wall is of simple construction – a timber frame filled with bamboo latticework and covered with mud. Tokui's decision to clad it with pale-coloured mud from the site was an important part of his "nest" approach to the choice of materials. After consulting a local plasterer about the practicality of employing mud, Tokui followed his advice to add ground oyster shells to strengthen it.

However, there was a further reason for making a wall that connects house and garden. "I was thinking of the relationship between Japanese tradition and the present," Tokui explains. "I respect old architecture, but many of its aspects are just too uncomfortable for modern living." Nevertheless, to show the value he places on the building practices of the past, he incorporated in this house a *doma* – an earthen floor that was a central element of the traditional Japanese dwelling. He decided, however, to represent this in modern style as a vertical feature. Just as Yoshiji Takehara has revived the *doma* in the form of outside interconnecting spaces (see pages 56–9), here Tokui makes it into an earthen wall that enters the house from the garden. "It stands as a symbol of the evolution of the house," he says.

The wild, unkempt look of the upper garden is deliberate, and is exaggerated by the rough plank benches. Partly shaded by the dogwoods, these come into use whenever Tokui gives his students an outdoor lecture on architecture.

Directly in front of the house is a dense ground cover of dwarf bamboo grass (*Sasa veitchii* syn. *S. albomarginata*), carefully trimmed to retain an untamed look. This effect is enhanced by glimpses of rustic ornaments, such as this old water basin.

The living room, with its floor-to-ceiling windows, looks onto the upper garden, and occupies a segment of the circle enclosed by the earthen wall. Only the window breaks the sweep of this wall, which is symbolic of the connection between garden and interior.

Part pond, part fountain, but in both roles very restrained, the water feature looks as if it might have evolved naturally, by some sort of subsidence. The intentionally shallow water level allows the stones to break the surface. Stones of the same kind were used in the terrace paving, but here they are laid in a loose and irregular manner.

☽ ☾
The plan shows the triangular plot, sited on a steep section of a hill, which made the property less expensive than it would have been on flat grounds. Although the limits of the plot are close to the circular terrace, the cypress trees beyond this are on public land, and are "borrowed" for the garden.

woodland glade
design: koichi nakatani

In the wooded hills of Hakone, close to a national park with views of Mount Fuji, Koichi Nakatani aimed to capture the look of a small woodland clearing attached to a weekend cottage. He wanted the garden to look natural and untended, yet be under firm control, and, as the house would not be used full-time, it had to work with minimal maintenance.

The surrounding hills were all reforested after World War II with Japanese cypress (*Chamaecyparis obtusa*). The tree has charm, but, as with all single-species stands of conifers, the lack of variety makes these woods rather gloomy. Nakatani planned to clear a small seating area, pave it, and surround it with deciduous plantings that, to the untrained eye, would appear to merge into the woodland beyond. To increase the light, the cypresses had been cleared from around most of the nearby properties, but Nakatani felt that the combination of deciduous and evergreen would create a balanced and peaceful natural environment. He wanted to leave the impression of a "cottage in the woods."

Some levelling was required, for the small house and for the terrace, but there was no major removal of earth. Owing to the need for low maintenance, Nakatani settled on stone paving, which he laid in a circle, bounded on the uphill side by a low wall, also in stone. This stone, a brown granite from Fukushima prefecture, is particularly hard, and he had it cut into slabs small enough to carry by hand up the forest path from the road; larger stones would have needed a crane, and that would have meant clearing too many cypresses. The water feature – a circular pond, sunk below the level of the paving and partly filled with the same granite stones – is fed by a pipe from the house and looks simple and elegant.

For several metres around the terrace, Nakatani thinned out the cypresses by about 30 percent. This still left a fair amount of shade, however, and so he introduced various pale-green plants, such as the ostrich fern (*Matteuccia struthiopteris*), with its 1m- (3ft-) long leaves, to give the garden a lighter appearance.

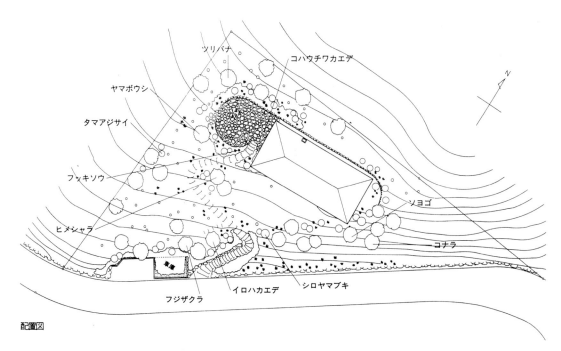

The edge of this dark and austere cypress forest was planted to include pale deciduous species such as the ostrich fern (*Matteuccia struthiopteris*), maples, dogwood, and stewartias.

a modern pleasure garden
design: masatoshi takebe

Covering 10,000 square metres (107,600 square feet), this is one of the largest private gardens in Japan, and was created for a client who wanted to enjoy a Western-style profusion of colourful flowers, while retaining some of the basic traditions of Japanese garden design. The designer, Masatoshi Takebe, whose company also maintains the garden (which, because of its size and the complexity of the plantings, needs constant attention), is one of the country's top specialists on Western plantings, and has a great enthusiasm for English gardens. Recent years have seen an increasing interest in Western gardening, particularly in flowers, but incorporating these into Japanese gardens is not easy.

The garden is called Ryogotei, meaning "a place for people to gather and enjoy themselves" – a name that expresses the theme of a fusion of Western and Japanese plantings. No expense was spared in its creation, and it contains some remarkable individual specimens. One large red azalea, approximately 200 years old, is probably unique in its size and condition, and is very valuable in financial terms. Among the most highly regarded of the fifty varieties of azalea in Japan, it is known as *kirishima-tsutsuji* (*Rhododendron* 'Amoenum'), and flowers red from spring to summer.

In combining the Western and Japanese gardening traditions, Takebe's design involves two kinds of juxtaposition. The immediately obvious one is aesthetic – he uses bright flowers in detailed combinations of colour, tone, and shape, as well as including traditionally Japanese darker greens and greys. Peonies, forget-me-nots, anemones, and tulips are among a total of more than 300 plant species brought from around the world.

The second kind of juxtaposition is conceptual, because Takebe has hidden some old Japanese principles beneath the immediate impression of colour. For example, he

Located outside the principal walled garden, and highly visible to guests from the driveway, is a large red azalea, one of the most prized varieties in Japan. Its size – it is a tree rather than a bush – indicates its great age of two centuries. Maintenance is demanding, and it takes three or four people working for two or three days to carry out the annual pruning.

A modest wooden gate set in a surrounding wall is the entrance to this spectacular garden, which opens to the visitor like a secret and unexpected world. This first view, framed by the roofed gateway, sets the tone for the rest of the garden, typified by winding paths and bright colour accents among the lush green.

This is the plan of the inner gardens, with the house occupying the top section. The main entrance to the complex is at the bottom of the plan, slightly right of centre, and from this a broad, paved path leads up to the house. Halfway along this path, a shorter path goes left to the gateway shown in the photograph opposite, and the principal garden occupies most of the left half of this plan.

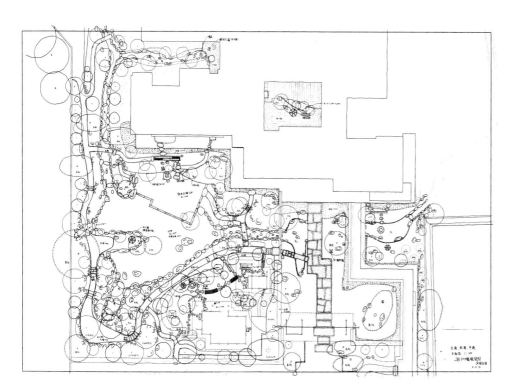

uses the Chinese-derived concept of *inyogogyo* – *inyo* means the contrast of male and female, positive and negative, while *gogyo* refers to the five elements wood, fire, earth, gold (or metal), and water. An instance of this principle is the siting of the waterfall on one side of the main pond, so as to project its energy towards the house; in fact, this was even considered too powerful, so Takabe placed a rock in front of the waterfall to absorb some of this energy.

Another traditional reference here is to a garden of Pure Land Buddhism, a style that appeared at the end of the Heian period (794–1185), when it was thought that history had entered a phase of false law. Such gardens were an attempt to create the Buddhist utopia as a means of salvation. Among their elements that Takebe has borrowed is the *nantei*,

Boulders, brought from many locations in Japan and set in mossy mounds, break the lines of the paths. They are important elements in the well-composed views offered at different turns.

A strong combination of Japanese varieties of azalea, seen here in full spring bloom, with the tulips and forget-me-nots more often found in European gardens, reflects the designer's aim to fuse the two traditions.

A rocky waterfall, carefully landscaped, feeds an irregularly shaped pond in the centre of the garden. The rock at bottom left has more than a compositional function – it absorbs energy projected by the waterfall.

The rear of the house is dominated by a tall Japanese cedar (*Cryptomeria japonica*), brought from Yakushima, near Okinawa, in the far south of Japan. In his fusion of international styles, the designer has created a very English bed of plants around the base of the tree, including violets and snapdragons.

a flat area immediately in front of the house used for gatherings. Traditionally this would have been covered in white sand, but the designer has interpreted it as a lawn.

As Takebe points out, it is important to distinguish between the different types of traditional Japanese garden. While, for example, the Zen garden, and its products, such as the dry landscape garden of the Muromachi period (1338–1573) and the rustic tea garden of the Momoyama period (1573–1603), featured great restraint, other styles of the past did use flowers. Azaleas are historically important in Japan, and played a part in many of the pond gardens of the Edo period (1603–1868). They were used in two ways – their flowers provided temporary colour accents against the predominant green, and, as bushes clipped into shape, they were often used to interplay with untrimmed vegetation beyond, as in the pond garden of the Joju-in temple in Kyoto. Takebe's use is quite different, as he makes them one of the flowering elements in a deliberately profuse composition. In the pictures seen here, taken in late April, they are at their most dominant.

In the Heian period, mentioned on page 152, flowers for entertainment played an essential role. This important early era of Japanese gardening was characterized by large pleasure gardens for strolling and boating, a style brought from China. None of these early gardens remains, but contemporary accounts record their use for poetry competitions and banquets. In the novel *The Tale of Genji*, by Shikibu Murasaki, a lady-in-waiting at court in the eleventh century provides detailed descriptions, such as: "The hills were high in the south-east quarter where spring-blossoming trees and bushes were planted in large numbers…Among the planting in the forward parts of the garden were cinquefoil pines, maples, cherries, wisteria, kerria and rock azaleas." Another passage tells us, "Since it was now autumn, the garden was a wild profusion of autumn flowers and leaves, such as to shame the hills of Oi." By drawing on an even wider, international, range of flowers, Takebe has here brought one of Japan's earliest gardening traditions full circle.

On the east side of the property, away from the principal garden, a second stream runs along a path. The sculptural qualities of dark volcanic boulder make it the centrepiece of a composition that again includes varieties of azalea, some late-flowering ones.

Spanning the narrowest part of the pond, a single flat stone carries the path that runs from the entrance gate to the house. In much Japanese gardening the sourcing of stones is as important as the choice of plants. Japan is rich in volcanic and metamorphic rocks, and the huge visual variety of these has no doubt influenced its gardeners' love of stone.

Curving around the west side of the house is a brick path flanked on its convex edge by a bed of azaleas. Here, it widens to encircle a single maple, set in a moss-covered mound. Takebe used grey paving bricks from a disused steel foundry to provide a restrained contrast with the flowers' vibrant colours.

Between the garden and the house is a slightly
sunken circular courtyard. Originally this space was
to have been occupied by a pool, but the owner
asked for a feature that needed no maintenance.
To create this courtyard, the designer chose *sakuishi*
stone, from Yatsugadake, as it retains moisture and
therefore supports mosses, which he planted.

shinto planting
design: satoru masaki

Shinto is the original national religion of Japan, unique among the world's major faiths in being an evolved form of animism. The *kami* – seen in some ways as gods, in others as spirits – are the powers of nature that are associated with its principal elements, such as trees, rocks, springs, mountains, and animals. Some are regarded as the nation's racial ancestors. In Shinto, therefore, the natural habitat itself is invested with sacred force, and this has had a strong influence on the Japanese attitude to plants and rocks – and consequently on garden design.

With this reverence for nature, the earliest shrines were built in wooded hills, and many of the most important contemporary shrines, including the Imperial Shrine at Isé and those at Miyajima and Miyazaki, are located in natural habitats, which are more or less isolated from mainstream Japanese life. According to Shinto mythology, the descendants of the Sun Goddess established themselves first in Miyazaki, on the southern island of Kyushu, and the west and south of Japan have particularly strong associations with shrines. These areas also number one of the few habitats in the world where the natural vegetation is evergreen broadleaf forest. In Japan, this forest is called *shoyojurin*, and is characterized by fairly dense undergrowth, a large number of species, and a lush green appearance. It is essentially subtropical forest with a resemblance to tropical forest, both of which lack seasonal leaf fall. Appropriately, the country's largest *shoyojurin* forest is close to Miyazaki, and for the Japanese this habitat is inextricably tied to Shinto.

This garden of a house in Den-en-chofu, an upmarket residential area of Tokyo, draws heavily on the Shinto legacy. The owner specified that the garden should require low maintenance and be enjoyable all year round. The designer, Satoru Masaki, responded with a re-creation of the habitat of an ideal Shinto shrine – a mixture of *shoyojurin* evergreen broadleaves and some plantings that are specific to shrines and their rites. Although Tokyo is on the eastern edge of this natural vegetation type, which needs warmth and humidity, the garden is suitable for it because of its sheltered location.

Above all, Masaki considered that directing the planting towards the Shinto way would add a philosophical depth to this small garden. He included a fairly large number of species, just as in *shoyojurin* woodland. Among the trees he selected are the evergreen oak (*Quercus myrsinaefolia)*, the blue Japanese oak (*Quercus glauca*), an ivy tree (*Dendropanax trifidus Makino*), and the chestnut-like *Castanopsis cuspidata*. Shrubs include Japanese aucuba (*Aucuba japonica*), Japanese aralia (*Aralia japonica*), *Daphniphyllum macropodum*, and two trees with special significance for Shinto shrines: *Cleyera japonica* and the *Michelia compressa*, a magnolia. The planting also includes a number of medicinal plants, such as the *Farfugium japonicum*, the leaves of which are applied to burns for relief, Japanese sweet flag (*Acorus gramineus*) used to ease stomach pain, lilyturf (*Liriope platyphylla*) to counter vomiting, *Houttuynia cordata*, used in Kanpo, a traditional Chinese form of medicine, to improve the body's metabolism, and Japanese pepper (*Zanthoxylum piperitum*). To add an extra layer of seasonal variety, Masaki also added a few deciduous trees and shrubs, including flowering dogwood (*Cornus kousa*), Chinese tallow-tree (*Sapium sebferum*), and Japanese stewartia (*Stewartia pseudocamellia*).

A side view of the circular feature of the garden from the living room, partly framed by a potted Schefflera. the two small stone *toro* lanterns were brought from Kyushu by the owner.

Overhung with ferns and lined with pale blue-green pebbles, a tiny stone pond at the far end of the garden is half hidden, evoking a secret spring. Natural water features are associated with the spirits that animate nature and therefore with Shinto.

house as garden
design: masahisa and tsuneko koike

Fast disappearing under the onslaught of apartment blocks, and rarely mourned in its passing, is the low-cost housing known as *nagaya*, which literally means "long house." The word "narrow" might better describe the house than "long," because these very basic, wooden-framed buildings are not large and are usually shared, the individual dwellings being divided along the axis of the buildings. While the *nagaya* dates back to the Edo period (1603–1868) as terraced houses in cities, most surviving examples date from the period immediately after World War II, when cheap housing was needed quickly. They stopped being built in the late 1960s, with the onset of the Japanese economic boom.

Where such dwellings still exist, as in this small neighbourhood in the town of Kunitachi, within commuting distance of Tokyo, they are little sought-after, but sculptor and artist Masahisa Koike saw possibilities in adapting one to become a self-contained "green" cottage – ordinarily out of the question in urban Japan. As he explains, while the Japanese ideal of a garden may be one that is an inextricable part of the house, bringing peace, calm, and a close sense of nature, the modern reality is quite different for most people. In a country with a geography that concentrates most of its population of some 130 million on the 30 percent of the terrain that is non-mountainous, the pressure on land continues to increase, and usually the first sacrifice is the luxury of a private garden. By Western standards, the Koikes' small home has no garden space at all. The veranda measures just 1m x 4m (3ft x 13ft), and the house is separated from the neighbouring property by a 3m (10ft) wide pathway that is used by both households. Undeterred by the physical limitations – instead rather spurred on by them – Koike took two steps towards greening the property. One was to use the vertical space by growing plants that climbed the walls and reached the roof, or hung down from the eaves; the other was to soften the lines of the building into a natural form by employing an ancient Japanese style of wattle and daub. The combination of these two solutions, with the help of logs, branches, and brushwood, makes this modest house function as its own garden.

❱

Planting troughs were created by applying render to shaped wire netting. Two tiers of these were placed under the eaves, allowing climbers and trailing vines to become established.

❰

The modestness of the house is masked by greenery, wood, and brushwood. Among other plants, there are hollyhocks in the foreground and *Solanum japonense* climbing the corner of the pergola. This rustic wildness contrasts with the surrounding suburban landscape, creating a tiny pocket of countryside in the city.

By enclosing the veranda with a brushwood fence
and a rough pergola of logs and branches, and
opening the interior onto it, the owners have made
excellent use of this tiny space. The home-made water
trough contains irises, hyacinths, and arrowhead.

The conversion of the *nagaya* into a "green" cottage took five months, a large part of which was taken up with drying the mud. The framework for the earthen render was woven from branches (traditionally bamboo would have been used, but Koike wanted a more irregular surface). This lattice was then lined with wire netting, both to provide a purchase for the muddy earth and to add curves and hollows to the wall. He chose a special earth called *arakida*, from Saitama prefecture, actually the fine silt from rice paddies used in laying traditional, fired-clay roof tiles. As it dries, countless delicate cracks appear, and the Koikes preserved this effect inside the house by not painting over it. The lower half of the interior walls, and the front of the house, including the veranda, were then sealed with a plaster mixed with finely ground pine-tree charcoal.

By plastering the exterior, Koike helped the vertical planting. Climbers predominate here, including cypress vine (*Quamoclit pennata*), *Solanum japonense*, morning glory (*Ipomoea hederacea*), and passion flower (*Passiflora caerulea*). Some climb the walls from the narrow perimeter of soil along the side of the house, while others hang down from troughs at the height of the eaves. A moulded-plaster water trough on the veranda is stocked with goldfish, and water plants such as hyacinth, lilies, and irises, while a rustic pergola of branches encloses the veranda. In addition to the aesthetic effect of a house enclosed by greenery, the plants and *arakida* walls regulate the temperature.

In warm weather, recessed sliding doors are pulled back and entirely concealed within the plastered walls, and the living area opens out onto the veranda. The same charcoal plaster used for the lower part of the walls covers the floor inside and out, and the final connecting element between the interior and exterior is a sunken iron sculpture by an artist friend, Kyoko Taniyama. Entitled *Tiles*, this consists of thin welded iron slabs enamelled white, one of them containing a small, round pond where plants grown in the veranda trough float. A brushwood fence above the veranda wall adds privacy.

The owner of the house, an artist who works in metal, has installed some of his smaller pieces just outside the veranda. This cactus holder alludes to the folding leaves of a lotus.

The earthen walls and cement floor of the living room are stained with traditional *sumi* ink, adding to the rustic atmosphere. Just inside the entrance is a tiny abstract "garden" with a pond and white pebbles. This draws on the *karesansui*, or dry-stone garden, tradition (see pages 18–21), but uses white-enamelled iron plates, made by Kyoko Taniyama, instead of stone.

The site, a steep slope at the head of a small valley, made it possible for the architect to design this wooden house in such a way that the asymmetrically pitched roof is at street level. This is the view of the planted roof that a visitor has when walking up to the entrance, which is reached by crossing a drawbridge.

A gardener from the the architect's office performs an annual inspection of the pots and their unique drainage system, which needs very little maintenance.

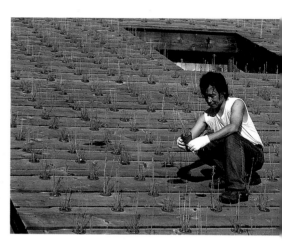

roof garden
design: terunobu fujimori

Roof gardens in the ordinary sense are no more unusual in Japan than anywhere else in the world – simply a normal utilization of space in an urban environment. However, when architect and architectural historian Terunobu Fujimori designed this house for his artist and novelist friend Genpei Akasegawa, he had in mind something quite different and more integral. The long, gently pitched wooden roof, which is almost at street level because of the steep slope of the site, is planted very precisely with 1,000 potted *nira* plants, or Chinese chives (*Allium tuberosum*).

Not the least strange thing about this unusual planting scheme is the choice of the plant itself. The Chinese chive is a staple ingredient of *gyoza*, the ubiquitous crescent-shaped dumplings that are a favourite dish throughout Japan and China, their place of origin. As such, *nira* is the subject of many jokes, in much the same way as garlic was once regarded in Britain. *Allium tuberosum* has a rather pungent odour, is full of vitamin A, is favoured by construction workers as a source of energy, and, all in all, is a rather rough, uncultured plant. It is one of the symbols of spring, yet it receives but one mention in the classic compilation of 4,500 poems known as the *Manyoshu*. Poor *nira*! When Akasegawa learned of the plans for his roof – highly visible, incidentally, to all passers-by – his first thought was "*Nira*, on my roof? And I have to pay for them as well?" But he could not object too strongly: "It's difficult to say something like that to Fujimori. He would just think I was being weak." Fujimori's reasons for choosing *nira* were its bright-green colour, and its hardiness. "This is a very strong plant, almost like a weed. We'll have no problems with it on the roof," he told Akasegawa. And when Akasegawa wondered how his neighbours might react, the architect reassured him, saying, "Don't worry about the smell. You get that only after it's cut, and the tiny flowers are fragrant."

Protruding from the main roof and capped with its own planting of chives (not seen) is a tea-ceremony room with a vaulted roof made of firewood – another of Fujimori's quirky and homely inventions.

The ingenious drainage system that irrigates the 1,000 potted plants so effectively is concealed under these horizontally laid planks, which serve as roof tiles.

One of the challenges facing the architect was to devise an unobtrusive and effective system for watering the potted chives that would function automatically. The roof is shingled with wide planks, and under the lower lips of these run water pipes. Fitting neatly into circular holes cut along their upper edges are the pots (below), the rim of each cut straight so that it can sit flush against the pipe to receive water (below right). To prevent leakage, the pots sit in glass cups.

So the plans went ahead, and Fujimori even insisted on involving Akasegawa, and his students, and on making an event of it. In the end, perhaps to the surprise of the owner and others, the house was awarded the prestigious 29th Japan Art Prize, the Nihon Geijutsu Taisho, in 1997. (The following year this was won by fashion designer Issey Miyake.) Roof as kitchen garden, house as art. This is not Fujimori's only foray into strange architectural plantings. His own house, Tampopo, or Dandelion House, is planted, roof and walls, with grasses and dandelions, which he tends himself with the help of a ladder. Other projects include a house with a pine tree growing from the apex of its steeply pitched roof, and another featuring a camellia. All are part of something of a mission to green urban buildings, and Fujimori experiments with ways of incorporating the living earth, to create a structure in which, as he puts it, "the building and the flowers are unified, or rather combined, in such a way that they support one another's character."

Fujimori's rather quirky approach to architecture – which, to him, inevitably means gardening as well – is, in fact, well thought out. The Nira House is a reinterpretation of *shibamune* – the old earth-and-grass-roofed houses that were once common in Japan's countryside. Fujimori remembers seeing one in Tohoku, and says, "If the plants you see are *noshiba* (*Zoysia japonica*), *michihatsu* (a small type of iris), *iwahiba* (a species of the perennial *Selaginella*), tiger lily, (*Lilium lancifolium*), or *nira*, you should consider yourself lucky, for you will have found a true example of this ancient Japanese roofing method, which is on the verge of extinction."

There remained some problems to solve. Fujimori knew the effect he wanted, which was more organized and architectural than a real *shibamune*, but he had to find a way to keep all these plants healthy. "I experimented first at my parents' house in the country, and realized that the most reliable method was to cut circular holes in the roof and insert into these plant pots, which would sit in special water containers." To preserve the neat layout of the pots, he devised a concealed watering system. Laid horizontally under the roof shingles are hosepipes, each one pierced with holes to feed the row of pots immediately below it. Each pot has a segment cut away from the rim on its upper side to receive the water, and sits in a glass cup that holds this supply. All 1,000 cups were made by Fujimori's students. The culmination of the roof-top planting was the communal erection of a homemade tea-ceremony room projecting from the top of the house. This vaulted roof of firewood achieves the same sense of the down-to-earth as the *nira* surrounding it.

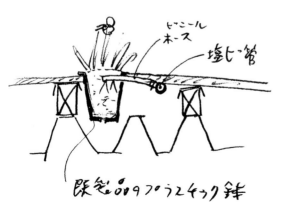

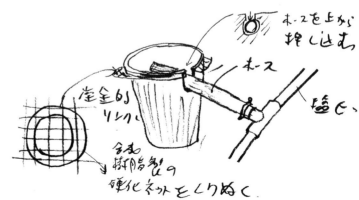

a profusion of green

design: masatoshi takebe

The garden of this house near Osaka occupies two sides of a first-floor terrace, forming an L-shape. A pathway winds gently from ground level to the first floor, where the garden includes a stream with small cascades and a specially constructed conservatory that allows for plantings on the roof and walls. The structural considerations needed for all this were made possible by the owner bringing in, right at the start, garden designer Masatoshi Takebe. While the house itself was built by the company that developed the surrounding properties, Takebe had the responsibility for the terrace, the slope up from the entrance gate, and the tall wall fronting the street.

Takebe, well known for his spectacular treatment of the large Ryogotei garden (see pages 150–7), is a great enthusiast of English gardens, and collaborated with Rosemary Verey in designing a garden near Osaka. In Ryogotei he added English floral variety to a Japanese philosophical approach to design. Here, despite the much smaller planting area of 70 square metres (750 square feet), including the path and paving, he followed his same feeling for an abundance of plants, but restricted the palette largely to green. He chose more than 300 species for their particular shades of green, adding an international variety to the native plants (a number of which are wild, from the surrounding hills and forests). He took a particular delight, for example, in including twenty species of hosta.

The house plan features a four-car garage at street level, and the house proper begins at the first-floor terrace. A substantial wall adjacent to the garage was required, and, for simplicity, Takebe wanted to face this with large slabs of stone. Ordinarily, these would have been very heavy, but he was able to find a granite in China that can be cut relatively easily into thin slabs. Behind this wall, parallel to the street, he planned the path and steps, rising to almost 3m (10ft) above ground and passing, near the top, the front door. Most of the stones for this came from another plot owned by the client.

The owner has added to the garden's collection of natural plants with a particular interest of hers – grasses and sedges. Covering the roof of the conservatory, these include the feathery squirrel tail grass (*Hordeum jubatum*). All are grown on Perlite, a siliceous volcanic rock that is used in its expanded, granulated form as a "soilless" mix.

A succession of boulders lines the path that leads up from the street, past the front of the house, to the terrace. Around and between these rocks is planted a huge variety of plants, chosen for their green colour, including hostas of many different species, seen here both left and right.

A small artificial stream winds across the large, first-floor terrace from the conservatory, which is walled and roofed with plantings. Lining the stream are native dwarf rushes and other aquatics, including clumps of Venus fly trap (*Dionaea muscipula*), just before the small stone bridge.

The inner walls of the conservatory are coated with a thick hygroscopic render made from plankton to maintain a constant humidity.

On the outside of the conservatory plants grow in a sticky mud. The small, fleshy leaves just above the rock belong to a button fern, the native *Pyrrosia tricuspis*.

One of the more unusual plants along the stream is the slender, long-stemmed white-top sedge (*Dichromena colorata*), imported from Florida.

A view from the upper floor takes in the terrace, with its plant-lined cascade and stream curving through the brick paving, and the tiered planting of grasses and sedges on the roof of the conservatory.

For paving that would look different from usual, and be lighter than stone, which would have been too heavy for the garage structure underneath, Takebe found oversized dense grey bricks that had been used for the flooring of an old steel foundry, and laid these in diagonal lines. Breaking this strong pattern is a narrow stream that has a gravel bed planted with contrasting aquatics, such as pitcher plants, Japanese rushes, including variegated and dwarf varieties of Japanese sweet flag (*Acorus gramineus*), and tall, slender white-top sedge (*Dichromena colorata*). Running water plays an important part in this garden. Starting with a gentle cascade high in the south-east corner, it then runs through rocks along the south edge to another cascade next to the conservatory, before crossing the main part of the terrace and reaching the top of the path. From there it is pumped back through pipes laid under the terrace.

The owner of the house wanted a conservatory, and this too contains a water feature of a waterfall over rocks, and a pool. Although both he and Takebe looked at English designs on a trip to the Chelsea Flower Show in London, they found nothing that suited the site. In particular, summers in this western part of Japan are hot and humid, and Takebe decided to build his own conservatory, in a design that would stay relatively cool. Also, while thinking about his idea of assembling a large number of species, he realized that this construction itself could carry more plants on its surfaces.

The roof of the conservatory is tiered, and waterproofed with acrylic. On granulated Perlite beds of granulated pumice, Takebe planted a rich assembly, mainly of grasses and sedges, including squirrel tail grass (*Hordeum jubatum*), pampas grass (*Cortaderia selloana*), and sedges such as *Carex morrowii* and *Carex flagellifera*. All of this needs to be fertilized only once every two years, and rainwater is drained from the gutter into a series of small pipes that drip onto the wall, where there is yet another planting. Here, on a plastic, woven-mesh mat of the type used for drainage in construction projects, impregnated with a sticky, black marsh mud employed in bonsai cultivation, grow ferns such as *Pyrrosia tricuspis* and *Lepisorus thunbergianus*, and ground ivy (*Glechoma hederacea*) with small, pale-purple flowers.

index

acknowledgments

The author and photographer would like to thank the following for all their help during the process of researching and writing the book:

Jun Izue, Shin Sato, Yasuko Ohtsuka, Yasunari Sakai, Jun Tamai, Yoshihiko Masuno, Maki Shimada, Atsushi Kondo, Masaki Shizuga, Kyoko Kanatani, Takao Okuda, Shu Hagiwara, Tomoya Murata, Koji Watanabe, Riko Kitayama, Masamichi Yoshida, Naohito Shirato, Hideko Takemura, Mr & Mrs Kaneko, Takao Okuda, Koichi Yoshida, Takashi and Toyoko Mikuriya, Takayuki & Naoko Houshuyama, Kazuyoshi Asakawa, Yoshihiro Obara. Suiko Nagakura, Amon Miyamoto, Akira Kaho, Mr & Mrs Mori, Mr & Mrs Kato, Mr & Mrs Ogino, Mr & Mrs Kazaoka, Koichiro Nakatani, Mr & Mrs Tobita, Mrs Sato, Mr & Mrs Kinjo, Mr & Mrs Nojima, Mr & Mrs Tanaka, Tomoko Illya Shimizu (Canadian Embassy), Shinji Nishizawa, Hisashi Asami.